PERSONAL AUTONOMY

Personal Autonomy

BEYOND NEGATIVE AND POSITIVE LIBERTY

ROBERT YOUNG

ST. MARTIN'S PRESS
New York

Library of Congress Cataloging in Publication Data

Young, Robert, *Ph.D*
  Personal autonomy.

  Bibliography: p.
  Includes index.
  1. Free will and determinism. 2. Autonomy
(Psychology) 3. Liberty. I. Title.
BJ1461.Y685   1986   123′.5   85-18424
ISBN 0-312-60225-1

CONTENTS

Foreword
Acknowledgements

For *Community Aid Abroad* and *Amnesty International*

FOREWORD

In this book, the author is very much concerned with the problems of liberty, negative and positive, although he thinks it better, in the main, to avoid such expressions. The reader may raise an eyebrow, but a considerable literature, under the rubric 'Autonomy', has already accumulated. In opting for 'Personal Autonomy' as a title, Dr Young is less concerned to achieve a novel effect, than to leapfrog the conceptual inadequacies attaching to a more conventional terminology. It is hoped that the reader may pay more attention to the substantive analysis than to the terminology employed to convey its sense.

It will be contended, of course, that one person's autonomy is another's subjection. Dr Young, however, does not view autonomy as mere freedom from constraint. More fully than heretofore, he seeks to show that conventional libertarian limitations upon autonomy are severely inadequate. He is able to do this because he regards autonomy as self-direction according to a life-plan which conforms to the individual's long-term ('dispositional') nature and interests. Given as much, dispositional autonomy may require the emplacement of constraints upon inessential or short-term or 'occurrent' acts of autonomy which seriously threaten that overarching life-plan. Traditional libertarianism, following Dr Young, takes insufficient account of the need for constraint, in varying degrees, to enhance dispositional autonomy. It is in this way that the author opens the door somewhat to a modified acceptance of 'paternalism' as requisite to any comprehensive notion of autonomy. The argument is both novel and important.

The dispositional autonomy which interests Dr Young is not so much a Kantian notion of self-direction derived from the recognition of objective and universally valid principles. It is a self-direction, rather, which derives from the individual being apprised of his or her own nature, and thereby being able to devise a plan suitable to that nature. What is presupposed, in such individuated self-direction as this, is not the primacy of irrationality. Rather, it is that a life-plan, devised for one individual, cannot necessarily be presumed morally suitable for all or any others. Simple moral universals find the going hard in terrain so broken and difficult. The earnest conviction that others should be 'forced to be free' (often enough associated with these universals) cannot find the going any easier. Given the centrality of personal autonomy for Dr Young, involving self-devised life-plans, the question must still arise as to whether and how we may assist other individuals in any quest for autonomy — politically, economically and otherwise. Dr Young firmly excludes the notion that we may best assist others by simply standing aside, negatively deflecting external engagement in the formulation of these plans.

If libertarianism is inadequate, which in various respects it is, it does not follow that socialism, conceived as a diverse bundle of solutions, will necessarily and unqualifiedly serve us better. But the problem of autonomy (or whatever we choose to call it) remains. Dr Young's book is probably the most readable, interesting and exciting attempt thus far made to delineate the logical and psychological nature, together with the moral value, of autonomy. He explores the sorts of limits that must be placed upon personal autonomy in seeking to promote a like autonomy for all.

There will be counter-argument to the present analysis: nothing could be healthier. What really matters here is that the author details a position that is summary, coherent, trenchant and relevant, cutting across the grain of much contemporary ideological prejudice. All sincere individualists, whether proponents or not of economic and other varieties of *laissez-faire*, will require to read Dr Young with care.

Preston King

3-20-91

ACKNOWLEDGEMENTS

Most of the research for the book was done while I was on leave and based at Birkbeck College, University of London, and Princeton University. I would like to express my appreciation to various philosophers for helpful discussions I had with them about 'personal autonomy' at that time. I would particularly like to thank Robert Merrihew Adams, John Benson, Amy Gutmann, Baylor Johnson, Amélie Rorty and Tim Scanlon who gave me helpful comments on early drafts of one or more chapters. When I returned to La Trobe, C.L. Ten kindly commented on a draft of Chapter 6. I was also fortunate to receive extensive comments from John Campbell, John Kleinig, Bruce Langtry, H.J. McCloskey and Peter Singer on a draft of the whole essay. My appreciation of their efforts is very warm indeed. My many other intellectual debts have, I trust, been acknowledged in the course of the book.

I drew upon earlier versions of some of my ideas which appeared in the following journals, namely: *The Philosophical Quarterly*, vol. 32 (Ch. 3), *Mind*, vol. 89 (Ch. 4), *American Philosophical Quarterly*, vol. 17 (Ch. 5), and *Canadian Journal of Philosophy*, Supplementary Volume 8 (Ch. 6). I thank the editors of those journals for allowing me to do so.

I want, finally, to acknowledge my appreciation of the practical assistance given to me by Marlene Forrester, Sandra Paul, Sue Pollard and Betty Pritchard and of the encouragement given me by my family and various friends.

Robert Young

1 INTRODUCTION: AUTONOMY AND LIBERTY

There can be no question of the familiarity of the idea of *autonomy* in the political sphere. We encounter it very frequently. It is, for instance, common currency in political debates in connection with nationalist and liberation movements. The struggles of the Palestinians, the Namibians, the Eritreans and others for autonomous statehood are almost daily reported in the media. The quest for a measure of self-determination in the political process is a basic one for non-white South Africans, Catholics in Northern Ireland, Basques in Spain, the Mujahidin in Afghanistan, for poorly off El Salvadoreans and so on. Because the idea of autonomy is so central to the world of politics it is common, too, in much less momentous matters than national self-determination. The idea has, for instance, frequently been invoked recently in relation to universities where cuts in public spending have threatened the capacity of universities to determine their own priorities.

The place occupied by *autonomy* in political thought is not new. Though as a term of art it has had something of a revival among political scientists since the French Revolution and, even more since the period of decolonisation this century (Buchheit 1978; Ronen 1979), its use in affairs of state can be traced to the ancient Greeks. But autonomy not only has an established place in thinking about political movements: it is also an idea that bears on how we describe the thoughts and actions of individuals.

It is to this matter of personal autonomy that attention is directed in what follows. Needless to say there are certain common elements between personal autonomy and state autonomy, and it will be useful here to foreshadow some of these common elements. The autonomous person (like the autonomous state) must not be subject to external interference or control but must, rather, freely direct and govern the course of his (or her) own life. The autonomous person's capacities, beliefs and values will be identifiable as integral to him and be the source from which his actions spring. Since such a conception of human thought and action requires more than just the absence of constraints and instead extends to the charting of a way of life for oneself and thus has a comprehensive dimension, it is more appropriate to frame the discussion in terms of autonomy than of freedom or liberty.

To place this construction on the notion of personal autonomy does

1

not give the term a radically new meaning. The Greeks sometimes applied the term to individual conduct (Liddell and Scott 1897: 253), and autonomy thus conceived has long figured in reflective thought as central to moral agency. Those who determine their own ends (at least to some degree) are recognised as having the dignity that moral agency bestows. Moreover, from the agent's own point of view, autonomy promotes self-esteem. These are points which have been taken up by writers as diverse as Plato (*Republic*, IV), Aristotle (*Politics*, VI:1), Kant (*Foundations of the Metaphysics of Morals*), by Kantians like Rawls (1971: 513ff; 1980), existentialists like Sartre (1965: 56) and libertarians like Nozick (1974: 31ff, 48ff).

The concept of autonomy advanced in this book draws on familiar features of the term, but is broader than that of some of the philosophers mentioned — broader, too, than the intention of other writers (like Mill) who use terms like 'liberty' to cover some of the same ground (Arneson 1980: 476). Thus Kant's account, which is probably the most philosophically influential, construes autonomy more narrowly as governing oneself in accordance with universally valid moral principles. A moral being is a law to himself. This is not because he follows his own desires. Kant distinguished the 'true self' of practical reason from the 'natural self' of sense and desire. The true self is self-determining in virtue of rationally legislating the moral law for itself. Because human beings are able to act on principles they have freely adopted they have the dignity and value that attaches to moral personhood. Insofar, though, as they act heteronomously, in relying on laws not dictated by the rational will, they lack such dignity and value. In stressing self-directed action founded on rational and universal principles, Kant's account of autonomy is narrower than an account based on action in accordance with a plan devised by the agent.

As well as being a long-standing topic of philosophical concern, the idea of personal autonomy at issue here has also figured prominently in fiction where the often tragic effects of its defeat has been a recurring theme. In, for example, *Nineteen Eighty-Four* and *Brave New World*, Orwell and Huxley have given us glimpses of what it would be like to live in a world where control over the direction of one's own life has for the most part been systematically eliminated.

Finally, in everyday life we acknowledge the importance of autonomy in that we lament its lack among those who are oppressed or who are severely mentally or physically ill, in wanting our children to develop in ways that permit them to exercise it and in the fact that our own self-images fluctuate according to the degree to which we can realistically think of ourselves as being autonomous.

The pedigree of the idea of personal autonomy is not in doubt. But pedigree alone cannot account for the currency of the idea in contemporary social and political thought. What does account for it is, no doubt, complicated. But the attractions of the idea are most clearly expressed by religious reformers, like Luther and Calvin, by a variety of Renaissance humanists (G. Dworkin 1981:207), as well as by liberals, namely that the capacity for rational self-rule is not the property of a very few (as Plato and Aristotle, for instance, seem to have thought). Thus it has come to be widely acknowledged that nearly every adult has the minimal capacity to decide on his or her system of ends and hence that there is no justification for any but an even-handed approach to the differing visions of the good life embodied in such decisions. This one development in the history of ideas goes a long way toward explaining the prominent place given to individual self-determination in contemporary social life.

There is at least one further point worth mentioning. Just as state autonomy continues to be accorded a high profile when it is under threat and needs protecting, so the contemporary prominence given to personal autonomy largely flows from the threats to which it is, or is thought to be, increasingly subjected. Those who seek to defend personal autonomy warn against the dangers associated with the development of public bureaucracies, private corporations, growing technological means of moulding opinion, and sophisticated surveillance techniques. I shall not in the main concern myself with the legitimacy of these fears. I mention them only because they, too, help to explain some of the current play being made with the idea of personal autonomy.

For the purposes of this book it will be important to recognise the inadequacies of the political model (of state sovereignty) for understanding the idea of personal autonomy. The traditional picture of the autonomous political unit is that it is marked by independence from the laws and governance of others. To be autonomous in this sense is to be sovereign or to have unfettered authority within a specific (political) domain. Under the influence of this idea some think of individual or personal autonomy analogously as independence from the authority of others (the state, significant institutions, other individuals). Autonomy thus conceived has obvious affinities with the 'negative' conception of liberty (Berlin 1969: 122), namely that to be at liberty is to be unobstructed by others, and with accounts of human rights as spheres of activity in which interference by others would be illegitimate (cf. Richards 1981). Since several writers (e.g. MacCallum 1967; Feinberg 1973) have called into question the distinction between negative and positive notions of liberty, on the ground that they cannot be analysed independently of each other, it may be as well to point out that I use these terms here only as marking a particular emphasis. Advocates of the negative notion take a less generous view of what constitutes an interference with a person's options, for according to them only the part played by other human beings in bringing into existence arrangements which interfere with those options is to be seen as restrictive of liberty. (cp. Berlin 1969: 122 with Frankfurt 1973: 83–84, Crocker 1980 and Norman 1982: 95.)

A central concern of this book is to argue that any view of autonomy that relies on the negative notion of liberty is too narrow. Some discussions of autonomy focus almost exclusively on *external* constraints and accordingly neglect those constraints which are *internal* to the individual agent (such as psychological barriers). While giving consideration to external constraints, it is necessary to correct this narrow focus. It is in pursuit of this objective that, in Chapter 5, internal constraints are taken into account in the process of investigating whether it is normally open to people to exercise autonomy. The blame for undue concentration on external obstacles to the exercise of autonomy is largely to be attributed to the negative model of liberty. Similarly, this negative model has had the major effect of tying thought about autonomy much too closely to an individualist outlook, particularly the so-called 'rugged individualist' outlook (cp. especially Chapters 2 and 8).

This individualist outlook is common in the West — as is evident from television serials, popular novels and neo-libertarian writing generally. Now it has long been held that there have to be restrictions on the exercise of autonomy where harm is threatened, or occasioned, to others. All supporters of the dignity and value of the individual share this conviction. But just how broadly the notion of 'harm' should be taken is less generally agreed. Those who keenly support the removal of restrictions on individual economic enterprise fail to take seriously the harmful impact this has on the autonomy of others (where autonomy is understood in positive terms as the securing of a large measure of control by these latter over the way they live their lives). This argument is further developed in Chapter 8.

The individual conception of autonomy has never sat comfortably with arguments for paternalism, where 'paternalism' is conceived as coercive or forcible interference with a person's freedom motivated by a concern to protect that person's welfare interests (or other important interests). It is sometimes claimed, for instance, that the autonomous individual has a 'right' to make his (or her) own choices, or should be free from interference with his own choices, no matter how foolish or self-defeating such choices may be (McDermott 1975; Stroll 1967). Such a position is confused in so far as it fails to keep distinct the occurrent sense of autonomy, autonomy of the moment, from the more important dispositional sense of autonomy, where the focus is on the autonomous person's life as a whole. Matters are not greatly improved if we restrict 'autonomy' to the dispositional sense and 'freedom' to the occurrent sense (as by G. Dworkin 1981: 211) — this for the reason that freedom is necessary for autonomy. Foolish or self-defeating choices can wreak havoc with a person's long-term, dispositional autonomy. It is very common in the individualist tradition to hold that it is only through the process of making decisions, making and correcting mistakes, and so on, that individuals learn to make wise and judicious choices — that maturity, rationality and such like are the *results* of autonomous choosing and doing. Now while it is largely true that maturity and rationality are the results of making choices (including mistaken ones), it is equally true that on occasion the protection of long-term autonomy may require placing restrictions on the making of foolish choices. The two positions cannot, accordingly, be incompatible. The libertarian and liberal traditions have, of course, generally been prepared to countenance paternalistic interventions where it can be established that an individual's choices have been rendered foolish because his or her decision-making capacities have been impaired. But this does not go far enough. (Closer consideration is given to paternalism in Chapter 6.)

It is necessary to argue, not only *against* the rugged individualist conception of autonomy, but also *for* a more positive alternative outlook. Those who support such a positive understanding of autonomy stress the importance of a person's *controlling* his (or her) life and projects. It is commonly countered that supporters of (positive) autonomy — who defend paternalism, the vigorous regulation of economic activity and so forth — are just adopting a totalitarian or authoritarian stance (Berlin 1969: 131). As well, it is sometimes said that this more positive view of autonomy carries with it a commitment to a 'real' or 'higher' self. This is because it is supposedly impossible to distinguish such a self from its phenomenal or surface level expressions. Talk of a 'real' or 'higher' self, despite its Platonic and Kantian pedigree, is thus alleged to introduce shoddy metaphysics. I intend to show that such views are without foundation.

The two chief concerns of this book are thus to elaborate an adequate positive conception of autonomy and then to uphold it against alternative conceptions. Only a positive conception of autonomy can do justice to its importance in our scheme of values and give point to its invocation by those who recognise the threats and obstacles to their self-determination.

Chapter 2 sets out the aspects of personal autonomy which have to be incorporated into any adequate understanding of it. Chapter 3 shows why personal autonomy occupies such a central place in our scheme of values. In Chapters 4 and 5, it is argued that the various alleged obstacles to the exercise of personal autonomy do not rob us of all personal autonomy. Given that we do exercise a degree of autonomy, the next three chapters proceed to consider the limitations that may justifiably be imposed on its exercise. Chapter 6 argues that personal autonomy may sometimes justifiably be limited for paternalistic reasons. Chapter 7 advances the position that harm and, under specified circumstances, offence constitute grounds for restricting the exercise of autonomy. Chapter 8 argues the need to restrict the economic autonomy of the individual in order to promote the value of community. The argument of these last chapters (especially Chapters 6 and 8) runs counter to prevailing opinion about the best means of promoting personal autonomy. The reader must judge whether I am right that prevailing opinion in these matters seriously misrepresents the nature and place of personal autonomy.

2 PERSONAL AUTONOMY: A CHARACTER IDEAL

I

The traditional view of the autonomous political unit is that it is marked by independence from the laws and governance of others. To be autonomous in this sense is to be sovereign or to have unfettered authority within a specific political domain. But it is not defensible to think of personal autonomy as simply reducible to independence, whether from the state, from significant institutions, or from other individuals.

One reason why it is not defensible to reduce personal autonomy to simple independence derives from the social nature of our existence. There are those who argue that *any* sort of individual autonomy is rendered unattainable by the socially structured nature of our existence, a claim scrutinised in Chapter 4. But putting this argument to one side, no promising account of autonomy can be usefully restricted to dictators (who are usually sovereign only over a restricted group of people) or to rebels (whether Hell's Angels or revolutionary terrorists) or to Robinson Crusoe. We require an account of autonomy in a social context, where individuals relate to one another via common laws, beliefs, moral standards, educative processes and so on.

Quite apart from considerations of the social nature of our existence, neither the individual nor the state can be conceived as autonomous along the lines of the traditional model of political sovereignty. According to that model, a political state remains sovereign, just because it is not subject to the direct governance or laws of others, even though it is economically poor. This is implausible. On the individual level, poverty severely restricts the options open to a person and thus restricts that person's liberty (Feinberg 1978: 27ff). Similarly, on the state level, economic underdevelopment frequently makes it impossible for states to control their own destinies even though they continue to make and administer their own laws. A truly autonomous state is one which is free from internal constraints, like a backward economy or lack of resources, and from external constraints, like foreign occupation or an economic blockade or imperialistic control of its economy. An insufficiency of resources (poverty), whether or not it is occasioned by the intervention of others, may restrict the options, and thus the autonomy, of both individuals and states (Frankfurt 1973: 83ff). Given that insufficient resources may diminish autonomy, and that such insufficiency is not always attributable

7

to human agency, it must follow that autonomy, whether on the state or individual level, is not simply to be equated with independence from the authority of others.

Instead of thinking of individual autonomy as 'freedom from' the governance of others, it is more appropriate to understand it in a positive way as self-government or self-determination (these, of course, being matters of degree). According to this conception, the more one is able to direct one's own life, the greater the degree of one's autonomy. Those who themselves determine what they will decide and do, rather than have these dictated to them by circumstances or by others, are autonomous. But the idea of one's decisions and actions being self-directed or self-determined requires, of course, to be filled out in a satisfactory way if these claims are to be convincing.

Freedom is only a necessary condition for autonomy. So autonomy involves more than just being free. This is easily confirmed: self-determination is hardly displayed in, for example, freely but mindlessly mimicking the tastes, opinions, ideals, goals, principles, or values of others. The choices and actions of an autonomous person are not just free but are also expressive of his or her own preferences and aspirations. In more popular parlance the autonomous person is his own man or her own woman. But as accurate as this picture is for popular purposes, it is not precise enough for present purposes. This is because it is necessary to distinguish the *occurrent* sense of autonomy, the sense intended when we talk of people acting autonomously in particular situations, from a further employment of the term to which we resort when we wish to make a more comprehensive or *dispositional* claim about the overall course of a person's life. In this second and richer sense, the self-directedness of one's life is exemplified by the fact that, in the main, it is ordered according to a plan or conception which fully expresses one's own will. The term 'plan' is here intended to refer merely to whatever it is that a person broadly wants to do in and with his or her life — thus covering career, life-style, dominant pursuits and the like, not some inflexible or unchanging set of goals. People can and do radically alter the courses of their lives without giving up their autonomy. Autonomy relates most importantly, then, to the comprehensive or controlling interests in people's lives. It is basically only this dispositional or comprehensive personal autonomy which enables an individual to enjoy a life that is unified, orderly, and free from self-defeating conflict over fundamentals. That is not to dismiss occurrent autonomy as uninteresting or unimportant. It will figure at various times in the discussion. But judgements of autonomy are predominantly judgements about dispositional autonomy.

In sum, the degree to which an individual's *life* is self-directed turns on whether that individual orders his or her life according to a plan or conception which expresses and unifies his or her choices.

Demands for self-determination by nations under colonial rule, or by sections within nations seeking some say in the affairs of their nation, have traditionally been held to arise out of the feeling that the nation or the section is oppressed or discriminated against. Self-determination on this account, whether national or sub-national, amounts to *liberation*. But liberation, understood in the negative sense, cannot constitute the whole story. While institutional arrangements of various kinds may well *undermine* autonomy, it does not follow that the adjustment of these arrangements will necessarily *confer* autonomy. One may well and rightly argue (as for example with Richard Arneson 1980: 475f) that anti-abortion laws can restrict a woman's freedom and thereby her autonomy. But the repeal of such laws (contra Arneson) will not of itself make her autonomous. Of course, the repeal of anti-abortion laws may provide scope for the pursuit of a particular life-plan by a woman which would otherwise be denied her. But from there it is over to her — for the most part anyway. Autonomy has to be worked for.

That is why individual autonomy, as it has figured in recent discussions, has been construed by philosophers as a *character ideal* or *virtue*. Such a construction is clearly linked with the Kantian tradition (as well as with the Rousseauian). Within these traditions, regulating one's own life is considered a virtue. But the conception of this virtue is expressed in divergent ways by different observers.

For some, autonomy underpins our conception of ourselves as moral agents; it is that expression of moral nature which consists in making our decisions and actions intelligibly our own through rational reflection; autonomy is growth toward an ideal of character, the rational development of a principled existence, not uncritical acceptance of the goals and values into which we have been socialised. (Cf. Benn 1976; Dearden 1972.)

A second set of commentators connects the idea of autonomy as a character ideal with self-realisation or self-fulfilment and accounts for the current interest in the concept by pointing out that we live in a post-Romantic civilisation which puts great value on self-fulfilment, valuing autonomy as a means to it (Taylor 1979).

Yet other commentators perceive the concern with autonomy as a way of highlighting the point that individuals can still will the good while under severe external constraint — opening a way, if not to self-perfection, then to moral integrity (Bettelheim 1960).

Common to all three positions is the view of autonomy as a character ideal or virtue. The differences between them are best thought of as differences of emphasis and focus. The three are not rival conceptions of the ideal. Such differences have sometimes obscured the agreed value to be placed on authoring one's own life and have redirected attention to related but more disputed matters such as the sort of social arrangements within which the ideal may be exemplified. Each of these three positions, therefore, requires fuller, critical inspection.

II

Those stressing the tie between regarding ourselves as moral agents and leading a principled existence have been most explicit about how personal autonomy is to be worked out in practice. Writers adhering to this position regard self-direction as an expression of the *rational* nature of persons. Self-direction is achieved when the individual subjects the norms with which he or she is confronted to critical evaluation and then proceeds to reach practical decisions by way of independent and rational reflection. In this rather Kantian approach, reason is linked with autonomy as the most valuable means of controlling one's surroundings. The advocates of this approach regard being autonomous as not merely being a chooser but making choices based on critical reflection. (Such choices might, none the less, turn out to be wrong or inappropriate.) Thus Benn, for instance, holds that the autonomous person must '. . . have reasons for acting, and be capable of second thoughts in the light of new reasons; it is not to have a capacity for conjuring criteria out of nowhere' (1975: 126).

Now undoubtedly reason has links with autonomy, because it bears on the capacity to discern truths and falsehoods, to make deductions and inferences, to formulate hypotheses, to empathise and to appreciate the central features in a situation, all of which may have a place in devising one's life goals, in devising means to reach them and in monitoring progress towards them. Not surprisingly many writers have, therefore, stressed the incompatibility of autonomy and unthinking submission to authoritarian religion and politics, or the acceptance of superstition and prejudice. As well, it is undoubtedly true that many a heteronomous person (say a skid-row alcoholic) does behave in a way that fails of rationality because qualities like judgement, reflection, planning and calculation are lacking. So on these grounds rationality seems a positive requirement for autonomy. None the less immoderate claims are sometimes made on behalf of rationality so that it becomes necessary to specify, both more fully and carefully, the place of rationality in the autonomous person's make-up.

Sometimes rationality is made too much a philosopher's plaything, either because logical calculation is made too big a part of cognition (as certain remarks of Neely 1974 suggest) or because the cognitive element is stressed at the expense of the affective (Barrow 1975: ch. 8; Dearden 1975). It is as well to remember that even the most autonomous of people do not generally act in the manner of profit-maximising firms.

Benn (1975) gives rational choice a central place in autonomy because it is crucial to the creative, conscious search for coherence that distinguishes the autonomous person from the heteronomous. Occasionally this suggests the autonomous person to be engaged in an unduly self-conscious and 'still-continuing process of criticism and re-evaluation' (124). But Benn later overturns this impression by making it plain that continuous ratiocination is not demanded for *all* principles and values, requiring only that the autonomous individual 'be alive to, and disposed to resolve by rational reflection and decision, incoherences in the complex tradition he has internalized' (128). In light of this remark and others (e.g. 126ff) it is not even necessary that the autonomous person's choice be rational (*pace* Benson 1983: 5), only that that person be prepared to revise false beliefs or poor choices when further evidence arises which implies that such beliefs are false or the choices poor. This is as well because much practical reasoning is not like providing a logical proof nor is it marked by the sort of giving of reasons that a judge is called upon to produce in support of his judgements (Hampshire 1978). It is more a matter of envisaging goals and determining the appropriate means to achieving them. This will involve the intellect to the extent that goals need to be made consistent or defended and appropriate means discovered, but rationality as conceived here is less intellectual than practical (cf. Rawls 1971: 408f).

On the matter of cognition being stressed at the expense of the affective element, the portrayal of reason as locked in mortal combat with unruly emotion needs to be resisted. If anything, the opposition to reason comes more from complacency and habit than from emotion. Moreover, for most of us at some time or other, tuning in only to the cognitive aspects of our natures is liable to restrict rather than enhance our occurrent autonomy (and perhaps thereby our dispositional autonomy) by precluding adventurousness and bolstering inhibitions.

Yet another example of the way in which reason may assume too considerable a place in the scheme of things is provided in an article by Ladenson (1975). His characterisation of reason makes it cover cognition (roughly, choosing and acting wisely) *and* volition (roughly, strength of will). If reason is thus characterised who could doubt its all-pervading significance?

In brief, reason should neither be construed too imperialistically nor made to appear like a taskmaster (demanding of us constant self-evaluation). It will now be in order to spell out its proper place in relation to autonomy.

Depending on the magnitude of their mistakes, those who draw invalid inferences or make use of incomplete or partially reliable information are likely to suffer in their overall autonomy from these failures in rationality. So not being seriously irrational does seem to be necessary for autonomy. When one tries to put the point more positively, matters are not as straightforward: there are ways of exercising autonomy, of directing one's own life as one would prefer, which do not depend on a highly developed capacity for calculation, penetrating logical analysis or any of the other trappings of a forensic approach to reasoning. Even so, being rational can be seen as significant in the following two positive ways. First, it brings coherence into the relationship between a person's general purposes and his or her particular actions. Some degree of understanding of this relationship will be needed to ensure that actions performed on particular occasions do not seriously thwart or impede more dispositional concerns. Second, and more importantly, perhaps, rationality equips a person to assess critically the advice tendered by others, an increasingly important safeguard given the extent to which we are reliant on the testimony of others about matters of great moment like health, welfare, education, economic and political affairs and so on.

The notion of autonomy as a character ideal is very close to the surface here because, as John Benson has remarked (1983: 5f), those who fall short of this ideal by over-dependence on the support, prompting and advice of others are regarded as credulous, gullible or too compliant (and hence as having defects of character). Autonomous persons, then, do not accept what they are told without any reason, or with too little reason to regard the testimony as reliable. (Cp. Downie and Telfer 1971; G. Dworkin 1978.) That does not mean that such persons will be arrogantly self-reliant. In some matters (*pace* Wilson 1977: ch. 7), we are better off drawing on information supplied by others when we know them to be reliably informed and not of a mind to take advantage of our disadvantage. It is, however, quite compatible with recognising the limits of one's competence to refuse to accept what one has reason to regard as unreliable. Benson (1983: 8) puts the point very well:

To be autonomous in [the intellectual] sphere is to put oneself in the best position to answer for the reliability of one's beliefs. It is to be in charge of one's epistemic life.

So where a matter is still 'up for grabs', or where the evidence is so readily available that only laziness could stand in the road of taking stock of it, or where there is antecedent ground for doubting the impartiality of a particular investigation or a source of information, autonomous persons must quite literally make up their own minds in light of the total available evidence. Not for nothing is there a notion of responsibility for one's beliefs — witness our attitude to soldiers who seek protection under the umbrella of 'acting on superior orders' when they ought to have questioned such orders. Nor is such responsibility for beliefs confined to beliefs about moral matters. Responsibility for one's beliefs is quite general (Stocker 1982). Indeed it is the heart of the idea of intellectual autonomy.

With these points in place, it is clear why proponents of the first of our character ideal conceptions of autonomy have argued for a close connection between autonomy conceived as the adoption of rationally chosen goals and concerns and the nature of persons as moral beings. For, they contend, where one's projects or enterprises are the point of one's actions others ought to respect these actions. Benn (1975: 129, his emphasis) puts it as follows:

> . . . the principles by which the autonomous man governs his life make his decisions consistent and intelligible to him as his own; for they *constitute* the personality he recognises as the one he has made his own. His actions, in instantiating his principles, thus express his own moral nature.

These points certainly fit with a Kantian outlook on individual autonomy wherein persons who form independent opinions, and chart their lives accordingly, in the process constitute themselves as fully-fledged moral agents. They become responsible for the course of their lives, moral agents with ends of their own. In being thus distinguished from mere things, from robots, they become worthy of respect.

III

The proponents of self-realisation as a character ideal underscore the critical importance of ensuring that the satisfaction of a person's desires do not run against the grain of that person's basic purposes. On this view, humans are purposive beings. Hence the recognition of some of an agent's dispositions, allegiances or goals as central to what he is or wants to be (by contrast with others that are not) is regarded as fundamental to the process of self-fulfilment, since the former will be intimately connected with the agent's deeper purposes. It is plausible, I think, to see the capacity for making qualitative discriminations among desires and purposes (for making what Frankfurt 1971: 7ff helpfully terms 'second-order evaluations') as connecting up with, perhaps even being a constituent of, the sort of self-knowledge required to direct one's life in ways appropriate to one's aptitudes, temperament and so on. In a fulfilled life, the individual's largely inherited skills and capacities will be developed in ways that sit well with that individual's interests, values and tastes. The capacities one has undoubtedly exert a powerful influence on the desires one has, though it is as well to remember that desire can bring to flower at least some skills. But this influence is not unidirectional — there is in all lives a certain amount of interplay between capacity and desire. Such interplay is the foundation both for building up natural talents and interests and for extending an individual's being in new directions.

In those areas which are of prime importance for the exercise of autonomy — career, dominant pursuits, life-style and the like — we will be the more fulfilled as we cultivate the talents and interests that it is apt for us to cultivate. Feinberg (1980: 269) puts the central point with his customary clarity when he writes:

> . . . If I pick a career that fits my individual nature instead of blindly drifting with custom or passively acceding to the choices of another, then I have exercised my generic nature as a thinker and chooser, at the same time that I have promoted the fulfilment of my individual nature as a person with a unique profile of interests and aptitudes.

(One might compare similar sentiments in Mill, *On Liberty*: 263ff, and Rawls 1971: 426.)

For most of us, there will not be just one career, one major interest or one style of living which would be fulfilling. Indeed, the more fortunate a person is as regards the possession of an array of talents and the availability of opportunities, the more paths which hold out promise of fulfilment. Paul Robeson was a top athlete and footballer, a first-class scholar who was trained in the law, and a wonderfully gifted singer. For the likes of him, many potentially fulfilling lives are open, though, no doubt, his racial origins limited opportunities more than would have been the case for a comparably gifted white. Some fulfilling lives are fulfilling because they have a single focus — Rembrandt's and Jane Austen's were of this kind. Others are so because they combine many strands, as with Albert Schweitzer. Self-realisation or self-fulfilment, like autonomy, admits of degrees. Some lives are more fulfilled than others and some parts of our lives more than other parts (Slote 1982). It is consistent with this that a self-fulfilled person's life may not be a happy one. A person might not be content with what it is open to him or her to do. And, of course, things that happen to one and over which one has no real control might militate against contentment. This may well have been true with, say, Rembrandt, who experienced much personal sadness. All of these points need to be borne in mind.

Notions of self-realisation and self-fulfilment have often suffered from excessively vague expression. Perhaps it is for this reason that they are not presently much in favour among philosophers. But they do matter, and this is not hard to show. Let us take our cue from some of the comments made on this score by Feinberg (1980: 272ff). He argues that it is only necessary to reflect on what a substantially unfulfilled life holds out for the one who leads it, to see that it cannot be for the *good* of that individual to go on leading it (or to have led it). Any hesitation we have about accepting this point is, he suggests, likely to result from not keeping in mind the important distinction between what contributes to an individual's *own* good and what contributes to *the* good. According to Feinberg, an individual's non-fulfilment may be objectively for the good, but not necessarily for the good of the agent. To use Mill's terms, the person who does not follow his or her own nature, 'starves' it and causes it to 'wither'. This is largely true, but not unqualifiedly so. To be less than fulfilled is surely sometimes better for a person, where fulfilment brings in its train premature death.

We may now take stock of the position. Firstly, although it is generally best that every person lead a fulfilled life, it would none the less have been *better* for someone like Hitler or Stalin or Pol Pot to have had another (less evil) nature. Secondly (here I wholeheartedly agree with Feinberg) even if the life of a Hitler, or Stalin, or Pol Pot be fulfilled, it does not follow that it is better all things considered that it be fulfilled. This second matter is one to which more detailed attention is given in the next chapter, concerning the relation between autonomy and other values that sometimes compete with it. Suffice it to say for the moment, despite the value of autonomy and the self-fulfilment normally associated with it, that other values sometimes take precedence.

IV

Now to the third or self-perfectionist account of the character ideal conception. Bruno Bettelheim (1960) provides a fascinating account of the effect on various personality types of imprisonment under the Nazis. He indicates that there were two ways in which individuals continued to exercise a significant degree of autonomy, despite the constraints with which they were faced. There were those who did so by first coming to understand through critical reflection the particular aspects of their situation which posed a threat to their autonomy. Armed with this understanding, they put great effort into the struggle to survive and to maintain their integrity. These prisoners exemplify very well several of the positive requirements for autonomy (to be discussed more fully in Chapter 4 below). In addition to exercising that degree of rationality needed by those who would exercise autonomy, they had sufficient self-knowledge to see how others were seeking to play on their weaknesses and manipulate them (cf. Rudinow 1978), as well as to resolve to carry through their perforce limited plans and purposes. The strength of will needed in their particular circumstances had to be harnessed with courage, perseverance and so on for them to survive in any degree as autonomous people.

As well as this group, who were mainly political prisoners, many of them communists, there was a second group whose members managed to hang on to their integrity. These were the Jehovah's Witnesses. In spite of the fact that their conscientious work-habits resulted in their being put in authority over other prisoners, giving them greater scope to 'feather their own nests', they steadfastly refused to do so. Alone of all those put in such positions, they did not use them to abuse or mistreat their fellow prisoners. They had, it seems, an inner strength that derived from their having resolutely determined to abide by standards they had previously followed. What is interestingly different about these men is that it seems unlikely from what we know of Jehovah's Witnesses in general that they could realistically be thought of as exponents of the articulate and critical ideal advanced, for instance, by Benn (1975) as necessary for autonomy. Benn supposes that they would qualify as autarchic, not as autonomous (127f). But however dimly we regard the inculcatory processes which led them to internalise the set of values they followed, and however unreasoning their continued adherence to those values may appear to us, in their conduct they clearly made them their own. That they violate the notion of rationality endorsed by philosophers, namely the critical defence of one's principles by reference to relevant evidence, does not license us to consider them as heteronomous (cp. Benson 1983). Their resolute efforts to will what they saw as the good, qualify them as autonomous to a significant degree. This remains true even though the Jehovah's Witness derives the idea of the good from putative divine commands. The one qualification, perhaps, is that the commands must have been so internalised as to become the Witness's own directive. Here then is a variant of the character-ideal concept of autonomy in which personal integrity (or, as some would prefer to say, authenticity) is the organising idea.

That such a conception should be admitted would be denied by Benn (1975) at least. Or so it seems on the most likely reading I can think of for certain of his remarks. Benn (128) alleges that

> . . . autonomy is an ideal available only to a plural tradition. However massive the personality integration and principled coherence of tribesmen and some religious sectarians, they cannot qualify as autonomous if they cannot claim to have actively made the nomos their own.

At first glance this may seem quite compatible with what was said earlier about self-fulfilment, given that Benn insists that autonomous agents must have 'actively made the nomos their own'. But the tenor of Benn's discussion of the Jehovah's Witnesses observed by Bettelheim goes against this conciliatory suggestion. As well, Benn elsewhere (1982) clearly and directly links his mention of the notion of the plural tradition with the Millian liberal ideal in which nobility of character demands 'a bold, independent and inquiring intellect, never closed to argument and experiment, of firm convictions and possessed of moral courage in action'. This model of the autonomous person is a very long chalk from the picture of the autonomous Jehovah's Witnesses that emerges in Bettelheim's study. But Benn's strictures about the availability of the ideal of autonomy other than in the liberal, plural tradition of which he speaks need not be accepted. We have already seen that rationality has an important, but not exclusive, place in the achievement of autonomy. Also, the case made by Bettelheim for thinking of the prison-camp Jehovah's Witnesses as autonomous is the more powerful in light of the fact that Bettleheim considered the maintenance of his own autonomy to depend very much on the use of his own reason and understanding. He was himself squarely within the liberal, pluralist tradition, not an opponent of it.

The association of autonomy with the pluralism of liberal society has become so commonplace that many readers may feel uncomfortable about being urged to sever the association. But there is no need for any such discomfort. Writers like Berlin have propounded the idea (supposedly within the liberal heritage of Locke, Kant and Mill) that autonomy goes hand in hand with a pluralist political and social order in which unique individuals develop their own distinctive interests. Conflict between these distinct interests is part and parcel of the very nature of individualism. There are some limits to the pursuit of individual interests such as that one should not be permitted knowingly to harm the interests of others. But it is the idea that each individual is responsible for forging his or her own life and making something of that life which is crucial. (Of course, individuals may find it advantageous to collaborate with others, but the advantage to each collaborator is what matters, not collaboration itself.) Rational autonomous choosers will thus pursue their own goals, modifying and revising them as they see fit. What one chooses will reflect one's *own* rational nature.

There are two further reasons for declining to identify this individualism in social relations with autonomy. Consideration of the first of these reasons will be deferred until Chapter 8. There it is argued that the individualist tradition, especially as it has manifested itself in economic thought, has, for all its noble rhetoric about the place of individuals, endorsed economic and social arrangements which issue in severe limitations on the life-chances of the great majority of persons.

The second, more minor, point, may be disposed of here: many major, recognised proponents of liberalism are not rugged individualists. John Stuart Mill, and some of his liberal successors, like T.H. Green and D.G. Ritchie, for example, did not mistakenly run together the ideas of human *individuality* and *individualism* in social relations between humans. They developed a view of liberalism at odds with that of other liberals more individualistically inclined (not to speak of their differences with even more extreme libertarians). Mill was, of course, no socialist in any strong sense, but in various of his later writings about socialism (e.g. 1963 Vol. 5: 747f) he shows a sound awareness that his ideas on the worth of the individual are compatible with economic and social arrangements of a non-individualist character. Others like Green showed an even more acute awareness that the individualist tradition has no monopoly on the idea of freedom (autonomy).

Green (1906) wrote, for example, that:

> When we speak of freedom as something to be so highly prized, we mean a positive power or capacity of doing or enjoying something worth doing or enjoying, and that, too, something that we do or enjoy in common with others. We mean by it a power which each man

exercises through the help or security given him by his fellow-men, and which he in turn helps to secure for them. When we measure the progress of a society by its growth in freedom, we measure it by the increasing development and exercise on the whole of those powers of contributing to social good with which we believe the members of the society to be endowed; in short, by the greater power on the part of the citizens as a body to make the most and best of themselves (371).

The conclusion to be drawn is not that autonomy is out of the reach of those who do not fit well in the plural traditions of Western society, but that autonomy is not the exclusive plaything of liberal pluralists or of libertarians. It may be exercised, for example, even by those who display a rigidity of conviction that elsewhere and at other times would disqualify them at *those* places and *those* times from being considered autonomous. Only an inclusive characterisation of autonomy will do justice to its various nuances. This conclusion, it may be noted, runs against much written on the topic by philosophers of education, who commonly place too exclusive an emphasis on reason, cognitive stimulation and so forth. (Cp. Dearden 1973; Crittenden 1978.) Autonomy is a virtue which can and should be cultivated by the many, not just the few.

The fundamental idea in autonomy is that of authoring one's own world without being subject to the will of others. And it is in virtue of this that our conception of ourselves (and of others) as moral agents is underpinned. None of this is inconsistent with others emphasising the point that the exercise of autonomy enables us to realise our own individual natures in ways which maintain our integrity. The positions we have inspected need not be thought of as rival conceptions between which an evaluative choice must be made. Each position develops an aspect of the fundamental idea of autonomy. It is when claims are made which suggest that autonomy is the exclusive property of certain traditions about human social relations that strong disagreements emerge. In Chapter 8, we shall return to such matters. For now, it is necessary only to reiterate that a broad perspective on autonomy can accommodate its various nuances as a character ideal.

3 PERSONAL AUTONOMY: INTRINSIC VALUE

It is surprisingly difficult to spell out the value of personal autonomy as a character ideal. Joel Feinberg (1979), for instance, writes that 'deriving and explaining the distinctive value of freedom is one of the great unfinished tasks of philosophy' (100). He uses the term 'freedom' which is commonly more restricted than 'autonomy'. Yet the meaning which Feinberg attaches to being a free person accords well enough with the comprehensive or dispositional sense of autonomy earlier discussed (cp. Feinberg 1978, sections III and IV; 1980). Much the same can be said of Mill's seminal discussion in *On Liberty*, despite the fact that he never once uses the word 'autonomy'. (See Mill 1963-: vol. 18, esp. 263–8, 277; Arneson 1980: 475ff; McCloskey 1971: 127; Ten 1980: ch. 5.)

Two views on the 'distinctive value' of autonomy predominate in the literature, while being rarely discussed in any extended way. According to the one view, the value of autonomy is determined by the value of the objects of choice (i.e. by what is chosen). This position is also sometimes put slightly more broadly as the claim that autonomy derives its value from other things which it makes possible. According to the second view, autonomy has value in and of itself, independently of what it enables one to do or bring about. On this view, it may be said to be valuable for its own sake, or worth experiencing or having for its own sake.

In fact, these two positions are not mutually exclusive. What they do represent are different primary focuses. First, the instrumental view that the value of autonomy is a function of what is chosen is a claim in the realm of 'act evaluation'. Second, the view that autonomy has intrinsic value independent of what is chosen focuses instead on 'agent evaluation'. If we accept, following the argument thus far advanced, that autonomy is best understood as a character ideal, then the second view becomes the more congenial (allowing that these admittedly crude evaluative categories do speak to something of philosophical importance). None the less, to value autonomy intrinsically is not incompatible with valuing it instrumentally. But what is said here is far too brief. The two positions require fuller development. Let us return, then, more fully and critically, to the claim that autonomy has only instrumental value.

I

That position on autonomy which values it instrumentally is frequently taken to be narrowly utilitarian, the value of autonomy being identified with the utility of the goods which it makes possible. These goods will vary from the promotion of well-being (especially contentment) to more ideal utilitarian concerns such as the advancement of self-development, the discovery and holding of true beliefs, the achievement of greater efficiency. (Cp. McCloskey 1971: 118–26, commenting on Mill, *On Liberty*, ch. 2; but contrast Ten 1980: ch. 8, who thinks Mill saw the value of these things to lie in the good consequences, like improved welfare, which they produce.)

It has been traditional to attribute a wholly instrumentalist view of the value of liberty to Mill. This traditional understanding is faulty, but it is important that we review it here. To begin, as a well-known champion of self-determination, Mill held in Chapter 4 of *Utilitarianism* that only happiness is desirable as an end. It is taken for granted in this tradition that Mill understood happiness to be distinct from autonomy. A similar instrumentalism informs the traditional understanding of *On Liberty*, where, in chapter two, Mill will be observed to enter the lists to argue for the view that autonomy of thought and discussion is causally necessary for the discovery and apprehension of truth. It would appear to follow, since truth, clearly and vividly apprehended, is a necessary condition for the realisation of the greatest happiness of the greatest number of people, that autonomy of thought and discussion is vindicated on utilitarian grounds. Mill is seen to mount a similar argument in relation to the development of individuality and of individual genius, particularly in Chapter 3 of *On Liberty* (cf. Ladenson 1977). So the gist of the traditional understanding of Mill's utilitarian defence of the value of autonomy is that we cannot in general make people better off (i.e. promote their happiness) by restricting individual autonomy.

These contentions, however, are not obviously true nor even very plausible. Indeed, it seems perfectly possible, by restricting autonomy, to promote happiness. Consider, for instance, the case of Huxley's *Brave New World*, where autonomy is on the whole circumscribed, its inhabitants being prevented from travelling freely, reading whatever they choose, expressing various opinions and so on. The exceptions in fact prove the rule: Bernard Marx is a rebel of sorts but has been well conditioned for all his intelligent oddness. Helmholtz Watson, perhaps, is free from some of the restrictions imposed on others, but is far from self-directing, which leaves only John the Savage and the world controllers. John the Savage is the nearest we get to a rebel, but that is surely because he has not been type-cast with the mentality needed for such a society. Given that these exceptions prove the rule, it can be said that radical closure of their options does not perturb the denizens of 'Brave New World' because they are unable to will to do other than what they do. They are happy with their lot because they can do as they want to, although they cannot want to do other than what they do. Their wants are programmed for them, but this assault on their autonomy does not take away their happiness.

Those who argue for the value of autonomy as instrumental, as narrowly utilitarian, can give no reason why we should not prefer to be in such a 'Brave New World', to be in a world where the genuine exercise of autonomy is diminished, and survives only as appearance, precisely in order to enhance the general happiness. That they can give no reason is sufficient to demolish a straightforward utilitarian view of the value of personal autonomy.

Some utilitarians will concede that, while the above criticism does hold for Huxley's 'Brave New World' (or for Dostoyevsky's 'Kingdom of the Grand Inquisitor' or an Orwellian 'Nineteen Eighty-Four'), it does not disprove the claim that, in the real world, happiness is always in fact best promoted by promoting autonomy. But this reply is unconvincing, for there are many people in the real world — not just in works of fiction — who manage to be happy while unreflectively following the dictates of their peer group.

Again, some would say that the argument leaves certain 'ideal utilitarian' (or pluralistic utilitarian) views untouched. According to ideal utilitarians there is no single goal or state, such as happiness or pleasure, which constitutes *the* good. The rightness or wrongness of an action is to be assessed in terms of the total range of intrinsic values produced by the action. The list of such intrinsic goods usually includes knowledge, love, beauty and the like. It will not, however, be for values such as these that autonomy is valued as a means. Rather, the relevant consideration here will be that autonomy is valued as a means to other goods, like self-development. This brings us very close, in fact, to the broader instrumentalist view of the value of autonomy. A common theme of those who place an instrumental value on autonomy is that it enables individuals to develop and pursue new aspects of their chosen way of life or to redirect that life in accordance with important new interests. Having such open options is even more valuable for those in the process of taking greater control of their lives, viz. older children, adolescents, young adults. For them there is an especial value in being able to experiment with life-styles, careers and dominant pursuits in order to settle upon a life-plan suited to their aptitudes, temperament and aspirations.

The difficulty does not lie in the suggestion that autonomy is a means to self-development in the sense just outlined, but only in the claim that such instrumental value exhausts the value of autonomy. Indeed, even in Mill's thinking about the topic there is a strand other than the traditional utilitarianism (and hence instrumentalism) that is attributed to him. We noted earlier that Mill's argument in Chapter 3 of *On Liberty* is commonly taken to be structurally similar to that in Chapter 2. If this construction were valid Mill would be claiming that autonomy is a means to the development of individuality (just as it is for the attainment of truth). Yet there are grounds for taking Mill in the third chapter to be defending autonomy as intrinsically desirable since he holds that '. . . It really is of importance, not only what men do, but also what manner of men they are that do it' (263). This strand of thought seems to conflict with his claim in Chapter 4 of *Utilitarianism* that only happiness is desirable as an end, which, for all its notorious reliance on the assumption that something's being desired is evidence for its desirability as an end, has fundamental importance for him. How then can Mill be read as defending the intrinsic desirability of autonomy without being plunged into inconsistency?

James Bogen and Daniel Farrell (1978) argue persuasively that when Mill talks of 'happiness' as the sole intrinsically desirable end, he does not mean to restrict the notion to a mental or psychological state attained when desires are satisfied. He uses it to refer to a composite of realised ends that encompasses health, virtue, liberty and so on. That is, he takes such states to be ingredients of happiness (or perhaps better, of a happy life). Accordingly, he can hold that autonomy may be desired for its own sake, even if it ceases to produce the mental state for which it was originally desired. As Bogen and Farrell (1978, 334) point out:

> . . . the fact that something, X, is necessary and sufficient for a man's desiring something else, Y, does not entail that once the desire has been formed, Y is not desired as an end (as something that is satisfying even without X).

On this interpretation Mill ends up very much closer to viewing autonomy as intrinsically desirable. And that is as well, because once it is taken into account that we are centrally interested in the value of autonomy for agent-evaluative reasons (because of autonomy's place among our character ideals), an exclusive emphasis on the instrumental value of autonomy has even less to recommend it. The instrumentalist view simply does not address itself to that consideration.

II

The second of our positions, then, to the effect that autonomy has value in and of itself, looks to be in the ascendancy. According to this position, autonomy is part of the moral basis of personhood. To the extent that a person is at the mercy of his (or her) urges or impulses, or lacks scope for actively planning and then achieving goals and purposes, it is the person's circumstances, not the person himself (or herself), that governs. Accordingly, the person's life will lack self-direction. In severely repressive or coercive circumstances (such as in the Nazi and Japanese prison camps during the Second World War or in some present-day psychiatric institutions in the Soviet Union) it is clearly very difficult for an individual to escape being subject to the will of others. But, remarkably, some do manage to stay in control to a significant degree, even if their resistance enables them to do no more than go on thinking for themselves. This in itself may be enough to preserve dignity and self-esteem. For others in very different circumstances, it may be irrational inner fears, misperceptions of the strength and significance of various purposes and so forth which tend to work against self-directedness. But to the extent that we are able to shape our lives in ways that we consider worthwhile, our self-esteem will be enhanced.

These claims for autonomy as providing the moral basis for self-direction and self-esteem are large ones and are rarely defended at length. A promising approach to their vindication has recently been revived by Robert Nozick (1974: 42–5), who makes use of a thought experiment with hoary credentials. He asks us to imagine an 'experience machine' capable of giving us any experience we desire once we plug into it. Our brains could be stimulated so as to make us think and feel that we are writing a great novel, or making a friend, or having any of the various experiences we desire. A large library of such experiences providing a veritable smorgasbord from which to choose could be made available from research into the lives of many people.

What, if anything, could there be about such a prospect which would make the idea of permanently plugging in to such a machine abhorrent? Supporters of the second position contend that it is the absence of autonomy. Just as the contentment of those in the 'Brave New World' has its attractions, so floating blob-like would seem to have something going for it, too, but what each lacks is the working through of a life-plan which expresses the will of the individual in question. To be content or happy is desirable, but freely to have been the architect and builder of one's contentment is better. This because, first, the sense of deciding and acting in ways that do not just reflect the impact of the world on us is important to purposive beings like humans, particularly as regards those projects that bear closely on our self-images and thus assume significance for us. Empirical support for this point can readily be found in the well-publicised and damaging effects which prolonged unemployment has (especially among the young) on the self-esteem of those affected. A distinct but not unrelated point is that bringing our own projects to fruition, not just passively experiencing their outcomes, also bears on our self-esteem. In popular parlance, we derive less personal satisfaction when things are 'handed to us on a platter'. Finally, presuming that it is only after making new choices from the smorgasbord that we would be able to strike out in new directions, then being plugged in to the machine would restrict possibilities for opening up new avenues of personal growth and preclude any radical reorientation in life-style or life-plan. Surrendering to the machine would restrict one to a particular range of experiences (in much the same way as happens with the taking of certain drugs).

To the extent that these objections to a hypothetical 'experience machine' are cogent, they reinforce the view that autonomy is crucial to our conception of moral agency. (For those who are dubious that much sense can be made of the idea of such a machine, similar objections would apply to life in Huxley's 'Brave New World'.) Autonomy — the business of genuinely choosing and acting so as to forge one's own lot in life — is an excellence which contributes to personal dignity and self esteem (*pace* Skinner, 1972). Autonomy is not just a means to contentment, since one may be content without being autonomous.(Cf. Haksar, 1979: 172–84, though he goes on to claim, incorrectly, as I think, that only a perfectionist can account for this intrinsic value in autonomy.)

In addition to such appeals to the imagination, there is at least one further way in which some philosophers have tried to show that there is value in having alternative choices, independently of what may be chosen. It is suggested that we should reflect on the judgements we make about the preferability of more extensive freedom in simple choice situations. The situations need to be straightforward if we are to eliminate the difficulties involved in comparing which of two significantly different actions requires the greater freedom, or which of two limits imposes the greater constraint on the exercise of freedom. Michael Bayles (1978:77ff), who thinks we clearly do prefer to have more extensive freedoms, and who therefore concludes that we consider autonomy to have value in itself, has offered several supporting reasons for his claim.

Bayles holds that one reason for preferring the greater to the lesser freedom is that, the greater the number of alternatives, the lower the risk of being dissatisfied. This is only true, of course, if the range covers the really important choices — the mere proliferation of choices does not as such promote autonomy, especially in its dispositional sense. Even with this major qualification, Bayles's claim will not do, because it amounts only to valuing autonomy as a means to avoiding dissatisfaction. Bayles suggests, secondly, that since one's actions become expressive of one's self as constituted by one's character and desires, the greater the options available the greater the scope for expressing oneself and thus for deciding how one's life shall be lived. If Bayles intends by this remark to make the point that, for those with an array of talents, there will be many paths open which promise fulfilment, well and good. Finally, Bayles suggests that even if one does not occurrently want what is available, since it is prudent to allow for changes in one's desires, the greater the number and the more varied the alternatives open to one, the better. Clearly, however, this is far from being always the case. Sometimes the wider the options, the more agonising decision becomes. We often wish that our options were reduced, a wish that may well endure even after we have made up our minds. But despite this objection, it normally remains preferable to have wider alternatives.

The conclusion is that autonomy is intrinsically, not merely extrinsically, valuable, that it is better *intrinsically* to be a being who shapes his (or her) own life. Moreover, this is *prima facie* a plausible claim. None the less, because the notion of the intrinsically valuable is not entirely clear it has had its share of critics. The object of the next section, therefore, is to provide a clearer picture of two distinct ways in which the claim that autonomy is intrinsically valuable may be understood, and to choose between them.

III

Two accounts of the nature of the intrinsically valuable have achieved some prominence. The first view is that the intrinsically valuable is what is valuable 'in itself' or 'for its own sake'. Since the intrinsic value of *x* is independent of its relationship with other things — it depends entirely on its intrinsic properties — *x* remains an intrinsic value even where there is no valuer to value it. It was this idea which G.E. Moore (1903:

92, 93, 187; 1911: 42) had in mind when he proposed his famous test for determining those things whose existence would still be judged valuable if they existed in absolute isolation. (Cf. Hancock, 1974:23f, who also charts the various changes Moore's views underwent.)

The second view is that *x* is intrinsically valuable if it is worth *having* for its own sake. Greater justice is done to this position if it is taken as a disjunction which incorporates within its scope a counterfactual claim. That is, *x* is held to be worth having for its own sake or, where it is not experienced, would be worth having for its own sake, were it to be experienced. Moore himself at one stage (1962: 94) held the unreconstructed form of this view but subsequently retracted it (1968: 555). Moore supposed that, to have a value, some agent must experience it. Accordingly, he feared it would prove self-contradictory to ascribe intrinsic value to any situation in which several people were having experiences worth having for their own sakes, since no participant can be held to experience the state of affairs as a whole. If, in brief, intrinsically valuable states require to be experienced, but no one can experience them, then there can be no such intrinsically valuable states. Even though Moore backtracked from this implication the view has continued to attract supporters, like C.I. Lewis.

Lewis (1946) offered a more elaborate classification of *value* to avoid the possibility of having to deny value to something which was not experienced, while preserving the notion that intrinsic value is a feature only of experiences. Lewis (386f) introduced the notion of something having *inherent value* where exposure to it could result in an experience of intrinsic value. This allowed for what was central to Moore's thesis, namely that value is attached to the properties of the thing — strictly in Moore's terms the intrinsic properties — while at the same time reserving intrinsic value for the experiencing of something possessing such inherent value. (Cf. Bailey 1979 for a similar device based on a distinction between latent value and patent value.)

Which of these two accounts of the nature of the intrinsically valuable is more accurate? As against the first, there is a serious, unresolved (and perhaps unresolvable) dispute about whether there can be value in the absence of valuers, a dispute, moreover, which cannot be resolved by appeal to a hypothetical 'ideal observer' (Beardsley 1965: 11f). Many of us oppose ecological despoilers, but remain far from clear that wilderness, for example, has intrinsic value. Accordingly, some philosophers have concluded that Moore's position is open to criticism because it would commit supporters to a form of objectivism about the intrinsically valuable. Such subjectivists contend that there can only be justifiable talk about value (including intrinsic value) when what has it is an object of someone's desire or choice.

What then of the second account of intrinsic value? According to von Wright (1963: 103) we can discover what is intrinsically valuable if we conduct the following thought experiment:

> Assume you were offered a thing X which you did not already possess. Would you rather take it than leave it, rather have it than (continue to) be without it? The offer must be considered apart from questions of causal requirement and of consequences. That is: considerations of things which you will have to do in order to get X, and of things which will happen to you as a consequence of your having got the thing X must not influence your choice. If then you would rather take X than leave it, X is *wanted in itself*. (von Wright's emphasis)

For Brandt (1959: 302) something is intrinsically desirable if it is 'desirable taken just for itself, viewed abstractly, and in particular, viewed without respect to any consequence its existence will or may produce'.

Both von Wright and Brandt stress that it is having or experiencing the X which is good in itself, the difference being that von Wright favours a more subjectivist account of intrinsic value, whereas Brandt leans more towards an objectivist account. But the earlier argument of this chapter, regarding, for example, the rationality of wanting to live autonomously, implies (with Brandt and many others) that judgements about the (intrinsic) value of autonomy are subject to justification. The subject of subjectivism versus objectivism, however, is not one upon which it is possible or proper to elaborate here. Suffice it to say, that in accounts of the nature of intrinsic value, what is crucial is the notion of *a value worth having or experiencing for its own sake*, not the idea of a value posited simply independently, or *on its own*.

For something to be intrinsically valuable (and not instrumentally valuable as well) we must desire to have or enjoy it for its own sake and not for anything else to which it leads. Since this is one of those cases where it is easier to see what *is* going on by making clear what is not going on, it may help to give examples of things whose sole value is instrumental and place these alongside some examples of things whose primary value (if not sole value) is intrinsic. Surgical operations, consumer goods and accumulated wealth are stock examples of things whose value is wholly instrumental. We value wealth, for instance, because of what it enables us to do. Its value is exhausted by the value of the things which it enables us to obtain. By way of contrast, beauty, health, love and friendship are desired because they are enjoyable in themselves.

Friendship, to take one example, usually also produces good consequences (and so it is instrumentally valuable as well). But it is not desired primarily for the things it enables us to obtain — it does not, for example, reduce to exploiting the 'old boy' or 'old girl' network (cp. Blum 1980).

Autonomy is like friendship in that it is the object of a rational non-instrumental desire, it is something which any individual might rationally desire to enjoy for its own sake. This is not to say that autonomy cannot also be instrumentally valuable, but only that its primary value is intrinsic.

IV

The contention that autonomy is intrinsically valuable remains open, finally, to at least two possible objections.

First, it may be said that if autonomy is intrinsically good we should expect it always to be desired, but that as a matter of fact it isn't. Second, it may be said that since autonomy is not always well used, it isn't even always valuable, let alone intrinsically valuable.

To begin with the first objection, it only follows, from the fact that autonomy is intrinsically valuable, that, *if other things are equal*, we should expect it to be desired. But autonomy is not the only thing of value and people will sometimes attach higher value to other things. Some, for instance, will willingly follow the crowd because they believe they will be happier doing so than pursuing a more independent way of life. For such people it will hardly be surprising that they prize other things above autonomy and so will, in the event of a conflict, prefer to give up their autonomy in return for the other things they value. (Cf. Berlin 1969: 170; Feinberg 1978: 30f.)

What of the second objection, to the effect that autonomy can not be intrinsically valuable because it is not always well used? Here, the intrinsically valuable must be distinguished from what is valuable *all things considered*. (Cp. Sidgwick 1966: Bk. 1, ch. IX, §3; Bk. 3, ch. XIV, §§2–3; Aune 1979: 4ff commenting on Kant's attitude toward well-intended actions with bad consequences; and Tolhurst 1983: 384; *pace* Beardsley 1965: 14.) The states of affairs entailed by the bringing into being or the exercising of something intrinsically valuable may be such as to produce disvalue and disvalue which outweighs that intrinsic valuableness. The exercise of personal autonomy may be viewed as intrinsically desirable or valuable given its fundamental place in the concept of moral personality, without its exercise on particular occasions being act-evaluatively for the best, or even for the good.

Opponents of the claim that autonomy is intrinsically valuable may still be unconvinced. The following further objection is readily imaginable: 'Is it not the case that the autonomy of a tyrant is of the same colour as his (or her) tyranny? (That is, the autonomy exercised in the acts of tyranny not that which the tyrant might exercise in the course of other morally legitimate activities.) And that being so, is there not a lot more to be said for the first of the two views on the value of autonomy than the position arrived at suggests?'

There is something enticing about this contention but, nevertheless, it needs to be resisted. We do judge the acts of the tyrant to be wrong, and the tyrant to be bad for performing them: thus the colour of the tyrannical acts and of the tyranny is the same. But in making these evaluations we are doing two things, not one. To the extent that the exercise of autonomy contributes to other things we value, it is a relevant concern but not a paramount one. Because autonomy is the foundation of moral personhood our paramount concern in valuing it is with the agent. *The tyrant is so much the worse a person* for having autonomously brought about evil. Had he little or no control over his own behaviour he would not be judged so harshly. But if, having the worst of intentions, he sometimes exercises his autonomy ham-fistedly and fails to make life a misery for others, he stands condemned all the same, his failure to bring about harm notwithstanding. Since there is no harm there is no wrong act. He, however, is not exonerated.

In taking autonomy to be of fundamental significance for our understanding of moral personhood, I have taken it to be an object of desire whose primary value is not that of a means to some further good. But it should be clear from what I have said that there is no implication in this claim that the exercise of an individual's autonomy may not at the same time introduce more disvalue than the value that resides in the autonomy.

4 PERSONAL AUTONOMY: EXTERNAL OBSTACLES

The two preceding chapters outline an account of the concept of autonomy, place it among our character-ideals and give an account of its value for us. It is time now to consider whether this character-ideal is one that it is possible for people to emulate (or, more weakly, to emulate in some significant degree). If not, autonomy will be of concern only as an attractive, but unattainable, ideal. Quite clearly, this is not how it is thought of by most of us. But there are those who doubt that people can exercise autonomy in any serious measure; they think that in no social context is anyone ever unconstrained by the will of others. This and the following chapter consider some of the impediments which it has been claimed block the exercise of any significant degree of autonomy by ordinary humans. The discussion begins with a reminder of the positive requirements for ordering one's life in an autonomous way, then turns to the 'external' obstacles to (or constraints on) autonomous existence.

I

In Chapter 2, it was contended that rationality is a necessary condition for autonomy. An insanely deluded person is unable to exercise the judgement, calculation and planning needed to order his (or her) life in a manner which is not fundamentally self-defeating. He may well retain some scope for occurrent autonomy and hence not need to be in care, but dispositional autonomy will be out of reach. Much the same applies to the skid-row alcoholic, to the painracked, terminally ill patient whose distress prevents him from putting his thoughts together in an ordered way, and to the very young child. Since the extent of our irrationality is a matter of degree, so, too, will be our autonomy. To the extent, for instance, that we are irrationally obsessed about someone or something, our dispositional autonomy is likely to suffer.

In Chapter 2, it was also contended that strength of will is a necessary condition for autonomy. Some people may find it quite easy to carry through with their life-plans and, thus, appear not to need strength of will. While this is true enough, there remains a broader sense of strength of will in which even those whose life-plans are implemented without effort or struggle have to possess the relevant inner resources or capacities. Accordingly, preparedness to carry through with one's plans and desires is necessary for the exercise of autonomy.

In addition to rationality and strength of will, self-awareness (or self-knowledge) is often and with good reason put forward as a positive requirement for the autonomous person. Such self-awareness enables a person to resist manipulation by others, or to overcome some of the inner obstacles (like neurosis or self-deception) considered in the next chapter. Nevertheless, the place of self-awareness among the positive requirements for autonomous living needs careful qualification. Techniques like aversion therapy, for example, do not depend upon the subject's self-awareness, but need not infringe his (or her) autonomy. Moreover, some barriers to autonomy are just 'outgrown' and so may not require the individual to gain understanding of them in order to overcome them. A neurotic fear of not being liked might disappear upon involvement in a serious loving relationship. Again, these points are explored further in the following chapter. For the moment it will suffice to say that self-knowledge should not be taken uncritically to be a necessary condition for exercising autonomy either dispositionally or occurrently.

It is misleading to speak of *authenticity* as a prerequisite for autonomy. The autonomous person's decisions and actions are not merely his (or hers) but his *own* (Dworkin 1976: 24f; 1981: 211f). The autonomous person's decisions and actions reflect his own concerns, not manipulation by others, social pressures, neurosis or an ill-assorted grab-bag of principles of choice and action. In this somewhat technical sense, the authentic person *is* the autonomous person. The previous brief discussion of Bruno Bettelheim's account of the autonomous Jehovah's Witness prisoners-of-war demonstrates the connection between authenticity and autonomy. These terms are at times employed to convey distinct meanings. But in this context they are used interchangeably.

The point of this account of prerequisites for autonomy is to show that, when properly understood, they do not preclude the exercise of autonomy by any except those who are genuinely constrained (physically, economically, etc.) or seriously disturbed or anomic. Virtually all of us, in other words, can meet these requirements. Not surprisingly, sceptics about autonomy have not claimed that the positive requirements are beyond most of us. They have alleged that the impediments to autonomous personhood are the 'external' and, very occasionally, the 'internal' blockages or constraints to which we find ourselves subject.

II

According to Joel Feinberg (1973: 13) we may classify the constraints that are of concern for human action as follows: external positive constraints, external negative constraints, internal positive constraints and internal negative ones. External positive constraints include physical barriers and coercive threats; external negative constraints largely consist of inadequate resources. Headaches, obsessions, compulsive habits, neuroses and the like fall within the category of internal positive constraints. Lack of ability or skill, ignorance and similar failings will be numbered among the internal negative constraints. Although we shall make use of Feinberg's categories, they are not to be employed uncritically. Thus, for instance, it is often a matter of perspective whether one chooses to call something a presence or an absence (cf. Bayles 1978: 74).

Feinberg's categories can be called into service to aid our thinking in two ways. First, and more briefly, Feinberg's proposals make it obvious that, while ridding a person of inner, psychological constraints may enhance that person's prospects of being autonomous, the operation of some external constraint may wreck those prospects. Second, and more importantly (for present purposes), Feinberg's classificatory scheme provides a helpful framework for considering the enormous number of ways in which barriers to an individual's dispositional autonomy may arise. An understanding of these constraints will make clearer when it is that individuals are not in charge of their lives.

On the whole we do not have much trouble picking out those external factors which impede individual autonomy. Cases involving the coercive use of physical force pretty evidently involve external constraints. Mostly such coercion is occurrent and hence will affect only the autonomy of the moment; but it can be ongoing and then it will affect global autonomy. This would be true for instance of a slave subjected to regular beatings or of the victim of a standover merchant, of a pimp or of an overbearing and vicious spouse. Matters can, of course, become complicated when more subtle ways of dominating or controlling others are resorted to: witness, for instance, the impact of indoctrination in the Hitler youth movement, on in the 'family' of Charles Manson. But even here the impact of such control is sufficiently overt and direct as not to leave too much doubt, at least in the mind of the critical observer. The going gets somewhat harder with cases where an individual forsakes all of his or her own aspirations to, say, care for a dependent parent. We may suppose that the person has been manipulated into a servile role. In some rare instances we may think, instead, that the person has forged a new plan of life, an honourable, albeit restricted, one. In these instances we will be inclined to see close parallels with those who live 'serving' lives, like Florence Nightingale's or Mother Teresa's.

This discussion relies on the intuitive distinction between being coerced and (merely) being under the powerful influence of another. The distinction is in reality far harder to draw than intuition suggests. It assumes some importance here, for what we have is a whole spectrum of cases ranging from ones involving coercion, to those involving 'powerful influence', through to those where autonomy is restricted in one direction but not in others. Without carrying the analysis too far, we must provide a working distinction between coercion and other sorts of powerful influence (Nozick 1969; Pennock and Chapman 1972; Frankfurt 1973).

Let us say that one individual, *R*, coerces another, *S*, (1) where *S* does what *R* wishes solely because *R* threatens to use *R*'s power to harm *S* if *S* does not do what *R* wishes, or (2) where *R* threatens to withhold from *S* some benefit that *S* has come to expect would be available without *S* having to do what *R* wishes. Clause (2) complicates matters a little by introducing the possibility that certain *offers* can be coercive. This is controversial, but given an appropriately vulnerable subject, some offers *are* coercive and thus operate as external constraints. (For some discussion and references, see Young 1980.) Let us say, by way of contrast, that where *R* exerts a powerful influence over *S*, this must be independent of whether *R* has power to withhold benefits from, or occasion harms to, *S*.

Even armed with some such distinction between coercion and influence, it may still be hard to determine what effect one person's powerful influence on another has had on the latter's autonomy. We generally think that rational persuasion, for example, leaves intact the autonomy of the person persuaded. With demagoguery, we probably would need to know about background factors (such as peer group attitudes). Likewise with hypno-therapy, the situation of the more vulnerable of two lovers and so forth. Whether autonomy is adversely affected cannot be judged in the abstract.

Fortunately, we need not spend a lot of time refining our understanding of which of these external positive constraints defeats or largely defeats autonomy. This for two reasons. First, it would require detailed consideration of the facts of particular cases. Second, and more importantly, since those who believe individuals do live autonomously do not need to believe this of all humans in all circumstances, there is no need to deny that external positive constraints sometimes do preclude autonomy. It is not this that is in dispute with those who hold that none of us is autonomous.

The only issue really is the reaching of agreement in any particular situation as to whether there are any external positive constraints in operation and to assess their impact (difficult as that may often be).

Can we safely leave the discussion of external positive constraints at this point? Not really, since there is an important argument to the effect that the socialisation of individuals eliminates all autonomy. That argument is most appropriately dealt with here. According to those who advance this argument, the 'external' processes of socialisation determine desires, tastes, values, principles (and thus indirectly some of the internal factors to be discussed later). The argument has a near parallel in the Marxian contention that ideology in, for example, capitalist society plays a crucial, distorting role in the formation of principles, beliefs, attitudes and so forth and through them, actions.

The autonomous person orders his (or her) life according to a plan or conception which fully expresses his own will. The objection to this position is that the socialisation and education we all undergo as children, adolescents and as adults develop in us the desires, tastes, opinions, ideals, goals, principles, values, preferences and so on which in turn determine how we will feel, choose and act. It is argued that each time we choose or act in ways that turn out as we desire, we strengthen the disposition to go on doing so in similar circumstances in the future. The upshot is, that our options are marked out for us well before it is meaningful to talk about our choosing to order our lives in accordance with a conception that expresses our will. It is contended that we do not choose our convictions and desires in anything like the way required by talk of autonomy, but that these are shaped and narrowed without our (the formed self's) consent. The conclusion is that we cannot view things from our own independent standpoint, be 'masters of our own fates', 'captains of our souls' or anything of the sort because we desire and value the lifestyles and life-plans we are conditioned to desire and value.

Irving Thalberg (1979; Thalberg and Pellow 1979) has responded to this sort of argument by suggesting that, while it is true that we are subjected to conditioning and socialising forces that rob us of autonomy (or of a significant degree of it), the removal or combating of such forces favours more 'natural' outcomes. For instance, most women have been deliberately taught self-effacement. But if this customary practice were ended, if the existing cultural conditions were deliberately altered, the more likely (that is, the more natural) outcome would be for women to be reared in roughly the way that men have been. The upshot would be a significant reduction not only in the degree to which women are subjugated but also in the extent to which they believe that this is how they prefer matters to be.

Those who advance the 'argument from socialisation' would doubtless (and with some justification) see Thalberg's concentration on deliberate manipulation as narrowing unjustifiably the extent of socialisation. Even what Thalberg characterises as deliberate interference with the natural development of desires is arguably not just that. Undoubtedly some of the socialisation of females into subjugated and supportive roles can be classed as deliberate, but other partial explanations involving reference to factors like the division of labour, physiology and sex-roles are widely thought to be relevant. Moreover, despite some acknowledgement from Thalberg of the problems attaching to talk of what is 'natural', there remains doubt about its usefulness even as a way of making a contrast with the present socialised natures of women. To suggest, as Thalberg does, that the 'natural' state would be roughly what holds principally at the moment for men, gives too little place to the effects of male conditioning. All who live in societies are affected by socialising forces. It is no great help to talk of an alternative, combative approach to socialisation as leading to more 'natural' outcomes. Thalberg is not blithely unaware of such difficulties, but he does not consider them in sufficient depth.

Consider a second line of reply, namely that the initial plausibility of the 'argument from socialisation' derives from making what are in fact only partial truths seem like rigid generalisations (Feinberg 1980a). Feinberg argues that there is self-determination even though the self that does the determining is not fully formed. He views self-determination as a continuous process which involves shaping by the self as formed till then, as well as by other factors.

Certainly it does appear that the *capacities* and *skills* we are able to acquire are largely, albeit not entirely, genetically determined (cp. Block and Dworkin 1976). Moreover, the capacities one has exert a powerful influence on the desires one has. So there is a sense in which the partially formed self (from very early on) contributes to the making of the developed self. (Feinberg oversimplifies where he claims (1980a: 149) that the standard sort of loving upbringing will act like water upon dehydrated food, filling out the self and actualising its inherent potential.)

The fact, however, that we, as less fully formed beings, contribute to the making of ourselves as more fully formed beings, does not of itself undermine the claim that we desire and value what we are conditioned to desire and value. (Feinberg appears to assume that freedom — hence autonomy — is compatible with determinism. This assumption cannot be canvassed here, although much is to be said for it (Young 1975, 1979).)

Feinberg — in claiming that the ever-increasing contributions of (the stages of) the self make sense of the idea of a self-made person — fails to distinguish (see Chapter 2) between a person's life being *his* (hers) and it being *made his own*. Feinberg's idea of self-determination as a continuous process of shaping by the self (as formed till then) is in some degree sensitive to this distinction. The difficulty is that the ambiguity between self-determination as conscious direction, and self-determination as simple adherence to initial loyalties, is not removed. Studies of political socialisation in children and adolescents, for example, suggest that concepts, information and feelings that are acquired early serve as 'filters' through which later perceptions must pass. It is well known that, in many countries, like the US, Australia and the United Kingdom, political party affiliations are formed quite early. The child usually learns to orient himself (herself) toward the utterances of party politicians and to acquire commitments on issues that are consistent with party loyalty. Adult political orientations which have their roots in early learning *and which have been adopted without conscious, critical consideration of alternatives* have been found both to influence behaviour and to be resistant to change. (Greenstein 1965). Yet there is a sense in which it is legitimate to talk of the emerging self as shaping political attitudes and commitments despite doubts about such attitudes and commitments being arrived at autonomously.

Political socialisation, say in the US case, differs in an interesting way from the case of the prison-camp Jehovah's Witnesses mentioned in the second chapter. There are grounds for doubting that the Jehovah's Witnesses adopted their standards and views by way of a conscious, critical consideration of alternatives. Hence there might seem to be a direct parallel with the present case. But there is this important difference: the Witnesses showed by their demeanour in the situation in which they were placed that they abided by principles which they had made their own.

Political socialisation will impose attitudes and commitments both unconsciously and uncritically, but without entirely predictable effects. It may encourage fundamental resistance to change. But then again it may not. Consider the circumstances of an already socialised late adolescent or adult who is confronted with events like a Vietnam War or a bombing of Kampuchea on the orders of the President. An individual who critically reflects on his (or her) hitherto unchallenged loyalties and values may gain an awareness of how what is valued came to be so. A strong awareness of the potency of particular socialising factors may lead to a conscious reshaping of political convictions.

Where we discern most clearly the impact on us of our socialisation (e.g. when we recognise that to satisfy certain important desires we entertain would necessitate doing things to which we are averse, or would involve risks or great sacrifice, like giving up career or life-style), we may accept readily that we have been socialised in such a way as to preclude our adopting our motivations *de novo*. But we may still believe that it is open to us either to make them our own by identifying with them in our reflective judgings or by rejecting them. Once privy to such awareness it does not matter so much how one came to have one's particular desires, but whether or not on reflection one desires to have such desires, that is, whether one matches up effective and reflectively preferred motivations. (Cf. G. Dworkin 1970 and 1976; Frankfurt 1971; contrast Thalberg 1978, but see also his more qualified stance in his 1979.)

Elements of the socialisation we have undergone sometimes hold sway because they operate largely unknown, or at least are unrecognised by us for what they are. Liberation from them *or* willing embrace requires a deepening in or a growth of self-knowledge. Once such processes in our socialisation are brought to the level of consciousness and, in being laid bare, become open to critical evaluation, the possibility is there for us either to free ourselves from desires we would prefer not to have or to identify with previously unrecognised motivations. When, for instance, we become aware of the way certain of our attitudes have constrained our thinking about particular topics, our whole approach to these topics may come to be seen in a new light. (Cf. Poole 1975; contrast Archer 1976.)

Two glosses are needed on these remarks. First, only the *possibility* of rejection or identification is referred to because self-awareness is at best a necessary, not a sufficient, condition for these responses. Among the other things needed will be the positive requirements for autonomy adumbrated in section I. Second, it needs to be said that the genuineness of either response will require that the agent's 'true' motivation be validated by the agent's reflective powers. However, as remarked previously, these powers go beyond the merely ratiocinative.

It is of some significance that we commonly resort to testing the genuineness of professed motivations by ascertaining the person's preparedness to follow through with his (or her) declared preference. It is just such tests, of what the legal tradition terms 'informed voluntary consent', which provide the theoretical underpinning for the 'cooling off' periods now customary in consumer protection legislation, in the making and ratification of wills and in proposals for advance declarations ('living wills') registering a preference for voluntary euthanasia. While such tests serve to protect individuals against giving in to aberrant (occurrent) desires, their premise is the responsible agency of persons. The autonomous are foremost among those to whom such agency may rightfully be attributed.

Can we rest content with this way of stopping the regress? Ultimately the answer appears to be 'yes', but there are at least two difficulties to which we must attend. First, a critic might urge that the only people who can reject or identify with previously hidden motivations, once these motivations are raised to consciousness, are those whose socialisation permits them to do so. Second, it might be objected that reliance on the idea of *identifying* with certain of one's motivations introduces a concept which is far more obscure than our ready use of it might suggest. These two objections require to be refuted — the first here, the second in the following section.

According to the argument from socialisation, the motivations, preferences, values, ideals and so forth that we have are not really our own because our role in acquiring them is largely if not wholly passive. Our first defence against this argument is to the effect that once our motivational structure and its origins are laid bare, there is a real possibility that we may no longer be subject to it. For the process of gaining evaluative self-awareness sometimes leads to *active* identification with or rejection of hitherto effective desires. The question is to determine how we are to understand the notion that people may be socialised so as to engage in self-scrutiny and then *actively* identify with or reject the motivations into which they have been socialised.

It is, of course, both possible and desirable that we should educate people to be self-critical, especially about their motivations. But the notion of educating people to be self-critical provides only a weak reading of the objection that socialisation determines one's capacity to reject or identify with previously hidden motivations. It certainly seems too weak to capture the idea of people being so in the grip of rearing practices, peer group influences and so on that the responses open to them are foreclosed once and for all. To miss an education in self-criticism at an earlier point in life does not necessarily preclude some later chance of availing oneself of it.

Rather than this weakened rendition of the claim, perhaps a more pertinent construction is something analogous to the 'hard determinist' claim of Hospers (1958) that some neurotics are 'lucky' in that they are capable of making the effort to try to be cured, while others are just 'unlucky' (cp. Bernstein 1983: 121f). This claim relies on an oversimple conception of socialisation. Socialisation is a complex phenomenon. It includes manipulation (right through from stimulation of stereotypic emotional responses to various selling techniques), rational persuasion (including therapies to which consent is given), and the use of external hindrances, rewards and deprivations. We have already seen that rational persuasion on its own is too weak. Much the same would apply to certain forms of manipulation (e.g. therapy involving hypnosis to increase tolerance levels in a phobic). But when we turn to other forms of manipulation and some of the coercive uses of external hindrances, rewards and deprivations, we are faced with models which are too strong. For these have little in common with the idea of persons developing their autonomy by way of gaining insight into how they came by their motivations (chiefly first-order desires and values) and then consciously accepting or deliberately rejecting them. There *are* people who undergo processes (therapeutic and otherwise) of whom it would not be accurate to say that these processes were only made possible by their having been manipulated or coerced. The 'hard determinist' illegitimately assimilates causation and coercion. It is necessary to avoid the parallel mistake of assimilating socialisation and coercion.

III

In reflective judgement, one may identify with the values one has been trained to accept, but one may also reject them. Where one reflectively prefers some ends or motivations to others, and deploys the will to act on them, one moves from the level of mere compliance, to that of authentic self-determination. (Dworkin 1970, 1976 and Frankfurt 1971 adopt a similar position.) However, to identify with one's preferred ends or motives cannot suffice to render one autonomous. A person's motives may be *his* (as Dworkin points out) without being his *own*.

Several points need to be made clear about this account. First, reflective self-evaluation is distinct from identification with one's values (cp. Watson 1975). Second, where an agent reflectively prefers a certain desire and then identifies with it, he (or she) cannot fail to care whether that desire wins out in competition with his other desires (*pace* Watson 1975). Third, identification with one's preferred ends or motivations cannot suffice to render one autonomous.

Though this last point may seem surprising, it is easily shown. First, one may identify with an end or value or motive because one was manipulated or deceived or because relevant information was withheld, making it impossible (in any such case) for the individual critically and rationally to review the situation. Second, one may identify with certain aspects of one's motivations because of a renunciation of independence (i.e. behaviour may consist in a slavish following of what family, spouse, friends and government authorities, *inter alia*, dictate). Even the process of identification may reduce independence and self-determination. An extreme instance of this sort occurs with those paranoid schizophrenics who believe they are other people entirely (e.g. Napoleon, Hitler or the like) and adopt the entire bearing and mannerisms of such models. Of course, the process may work for ill in other ways: the models may be undesirable and produce distorted values and objectionable behaviour. Finally, because we may identify with a certain occurrent motivation in such a way as to undermine comprehensive or dispositional autonomy, it is necessary to be cautious about the way we employ the idea of identification as a condition for autonomy. But even if there is no prospect of identification being sufficient, it may still prove necessary for autonomy.

Though the term 'identification' has an everyday usage it first figured prominently in psychoanalytic literature. Given the amount of attention that it has received there, and given that the use of the term in recent discussions of autonomy appears to owe something at least to this more technical usage, it would be foolish to ignore the efforts made in that tradition to make precise the term's meaning.

In psychoanalysis the term is used above all in the sense of identification of oneself with another person. As it stands this does not take us much beyond everyday usage. But in everyday usage little if any distinction is made between this sense of identification and any of the group of psychological concepts with which it overlaps like imitation, sympathy, mental contagion, projection and so on. In psychoanalytic theory, however, the concept, most notably following Freud, has come to be centrally important because of its supposedly integrative function for human personality.

It is generally agreed that Freud held identification to be the earliest expression of an emotional tie with another person. A boy, for instance identifies with his father as an 'ego ideal' — someone he would like to be, rather than something he would like to have. After infancy, the propensity to identify is carried over into new situations and may arise with any new perception of a common quality shared with some other person who is not an object of the sexual instinct. So identification is not simple imitation but assimilation. In his mature work, like *Group Psychology and the Analysis of the Ego*, Freud (1953, vol. 18: 67–143) distinguished several modes of identification. He sought to account both for the need and the ability of individuals to affiliate, as well as for the unconscious operation, the strength of motivation and the sometimes irrational manifestation of this need and capacity. But identification in the primal form of an emotional tie with the object (sometimes referred to as incorporation or introjection) remained for him the prototype. This insight has had enduring influence.

Freud's treatment of 'identification' went beyond imitation and involved assimilation. Still, he recognised the link between imitation and identification and this link has come to occupy a central place in discussions of the topic within the psychoanalytic tradition. The first thing to notice about it is that imitation (in the selective sense presupposed in the literature) is *active* not passive. Moreover, it involves some interiorisation. Each of these points fits well with the emphasis on reflectiveness in discussions of autonomy. But there is still clearly something of a step from imitation to identification. In what does it consist? Piaget, for one, suggested that identification is selective to a higher degree than imitation. To my mind, though, no one has better characterised the nature of this step than Richard Wollheim who, in a fascinating paper (1974), argues that in order to make the distinction between identification and imitation it is necessary to go beyond purely behavioural considerations. Wollheim finds the difference in *imagination*. What makes his discussion even more interesting is that he takes himself to be elaborating on Freud's own theory. The heart of identification for Freud, says Wollheim, is that the person centrally imagined is imagined *from the inside*, that is, empathically rather than sympathetically. This empathic imagining is achieved by making use of the beliefs, dispositional and occurrent, of the one identified with. But more, identification has an efficacy for which imagination as such in no way prepares us. This peculiar efficacy Wollheim attributes to the way in which we conceive or represent to ourselves our mental processes.

When these elements are put together we have the following account (by Wollheim out of Freud): to identify with another is to write a part for oneself, based upon that other, with a view to being carried away by the performance when one acts it out. Whether or not such identifications become permanent will be influenced, perhaps, by the extent of reinforcement (e.g. through repeated experiences of effectiveness, competence and boosted self-esteem) and by the compatibility between incorporation and the individual's formed nature and temperament. Indeed, as Wollheim himself suggests, while identification makes its first appearance in Freud as a defence mechanism, Freud saw that a defence which is constantly iterated conditions or constitutes the character and can thus be a means of fixing a trait or feature.

This then is Freud's prototypical sense of identification. Freud did, of course, as Wollheim recognises, put the term to other uses, especially in relation to those with pathological conditions. Much of the clinical literature on the topic has to do with neurotic identifications. Our understanding of the concept can be taken a stage further by attending to some of the points made in this clinical literature. Psychoanalysts claim that the identifications of seriously disturbed persons are clearly distinguishable from those of normal, healthy people. The former tend to be superficial, transient and rather wooden or caricatured mimickings and to fail to convey any sense of an integrated human identity (cf. Schechter 1968). The latter are more stable, more selective and more smoothly integrated into the rest of the personality (cf. Bettelheim 1960: 79f).

This suggested distinction between authentic and inauthentic identifications seems to transfer readily to less pathological, everyday cases. Observe the wife who surrenders to her husband's decisions in such a degree as to make nonsense of the idea that she lives her own life. Or take the minister who remains in the cabinet despite being deeply at odds with the requirements of cabinet solidarity on a particular issue. The wife and the politician in these examples seem merely to be going along with the decisions of others. In this regard their behaviour contrasts with those who identify with the aspirations or concerns of others but who manifestly are not just going along with the views of those others.

While this is promising, more needs to be said yet to make the contrast sharper. There is evidence that the individual who to all appearances identifies with some ideal or style that he finds uncongenial may display outward enthusiasm but be at sea in furnishing explanations of relevant phenomena. Thus we speak of someone as parroting ideas and actions rather than making them his or her own. The sort of imitation (sometimes, indeed, caricature) involved in such cases is exemplified by the student who writes essays and produces ideas for effect, who makes no real attempt to get into the skin of things discussed. That sort of imitation is a far cry from, say, the kind A'Kempis had in mind in writing *The Imitation of Christ*.

Consider the position of individuals living in countries ruled by dictators where the failure to conform may be severely punished. If in such circumstances an individual conforms outwardly while keeping his (or her) own counsel (i.e. goes on thinking for himself), he has not identified with the approved modes of behaviour, but is merely engaging in them. Those who through fear convert to the current ideology and close their minds to criticism of it, no longer daring to doubt its rightness, are in a different boat. Their identification, in turn, is less intense still than that of those who enthusiastically support the regime. A useful comparison, is Bettelheim's description (1960: 169–75) of the 'old' prisoners who identified with the SS and members of the SS themselves. Similar comparisons could be derived from Solzhenitsyn's account of life in the Gulag.

Healthy or positive identifications organise and integrate an individual's affective and cognitive states. Hence the individual who can, say, delay impulsive identifications is less likely to become helplessly dependent on others to give his (or her) life direction. Healthy identifications will thus be selective and reflective and, in line with these features, relatively stable. They will be smoothly integrated into the personality.

The concept of identification, at least as it relates to identifications with others, is not obscure. It involves imagining the life of another from the inside. The problem now is to determine how, where express identification with others is not involved, an individual's identifications with his (or her) desires can make them his *own*. In this one-person case the individual may, say, imagine himself doing some action, living some particular sort of life-style or pursuing some particular career. What is then required is that he 'stand back from' these imaginings, survey them and respond to them. The response might be one of rejection or of acceptance. But this extended process of imagining what it would be like to do or be certain things and then making a response to these imaginings constitutes identification in the one-person case. This is not to deny that there can be, or will be, conflicts between the sets of ideals with which an individual identifies. Where such conflicts and disharmonies among the demands on an individual persist, dispositional autonomy will be impeded though occurrent autonomy may often be managed. But this is simply a further reminder that identification is not sufficient for autonomy.

IV

It is now time to turn, much more briefly, from consideration of the impact on autonomy of the external positive constraints, to the consideration of the external negative constraints. While there has been significant agreement about the potential effect on autonomy of the external positive constraints, there has been something of a divide over the external negative ones. Nonetheless, the fundamental point to be made about them can be made very simply.

For those (like Berlin 1969:122; though see Norman 1982: 95f) who hold that freedom is freedom from the interference of others *and nothing else*, only the external positive constraints are to be regarded as restricting freedom. This is, however, implausible, whatever one thinks of the supposed distinction between negative and positive freedom. Suppose *R* to have substantial financial resources at his disposal and *S* to have much less. *R* is able to choose a life-plan which would involve him spending large sums of money on, for instance, travel, entertainment and the other desirable trappings of life. *S* is unable so to choose. Whether or not *R* chooses thus to spend his money, he (unlike *S*) has the option. *R* is to that extent better able to live autonomously. Insufficient resources do restrict autonomy. Hence it is reasonable to accept that external negative constraints may diminish autonomy. In the extreme case (as of abject poverty) they may even destroy it.

5 PERSONAL AUTONOMY: INTERNAL OBSTACLES

An autonomous life is one that is directed in accordance with an individual's own conception of what he (or she) wants to do in and with that life. Such an account requires us to think of autonomy as involving more than just the absence of constraints. A purely 'negative' conception (of absent constraint) leaves out the positive element of self-determination essential to an adequate account of autonomy. Self-determination is essential to autonomy for several reasons.

First, to be autonomous is not merely to have a capacity, nor the opportunity to exercise a capacity. Autonomy is an *exercise-concept*, to use Charles Taylor's phrase (1979: 177f). That is not to say that either capacity or opportunity is irrelevant to discussions of autonomy. On the contrary, as suggested earlier, to be autonomous requires the capacity to do those things which figure prominently in one's life-plan, the possession of certain positive attributes, as well as the absence of the sort of external constraints already considered.

Second, self-determination is essential to autonomy for the reason that persons who are otherwise free of external constraints may still fail to live lives of their own. The desires and principles on which they act may not be directly enough attributable to them. These desires and principles may be the product of socialisation, a socialisation undergone without any reflective awareness that it has occurred. Or they may have developed from the mindless imitation of the preferences and aspirations of other people.

Third, there is a strong connection between autonomy and self-realisation (or self-fulfilment).

To acknowledge these points is to make plain the need to think about *inner* obstacles to autonomy. If autonomy involves effective determination and shaping of one's life it can fail to be exercised because of inner obstacles as well as external ones. One can fail to be autonomous because of one's inner fears, because one cannot violate norms one has internalised, because one allows elements in one's nature which will not admit of denial to be thwarted, because of lack of knowledge or awareness of one's motivations, or because of lack of self-control, just as one can fail because of systematic bullying or physical enslavement. Indeed we can even appear, in some of these circumstances, to be doing what we want while actually frustrating the exercise of self-determination. This can happen where, for instance, what we want is liable to undermine our deeper purposes and concerns. It would be better were such a want to be repudiated. To satisfy it would not promote those deeper purposes which form the basis of the life-plan that orders and unifies an autonomous person's life and makes it appropriate to speak of it as self-directed.

I

It is a common and long-standing complaint (cf. Berlin 1969: 133f) against those who recognise internal, and not only external, obstacles to autonomy, that doing so depends on being able to distinguish the 'real' (or 'true', or some would say 'higher') self from a more phenomenal or surface version of the self. This objection has always owed a lot to the positivist temper and its disdain for anything metaphysical. But there is no need to saddle oneself with anything very controversial in order to give the inner obstacles to autonomy the place which their importance warrants.

Suppose *F* to have a passion for another person, *M*, and to have allowed it to modify her usual ideas and modes of behaviour. Suppose further that *F* knows, as do her friends, that continuing involvement with *M* will require of her that she forsake the values and ideals (feminist ones, perhaps) which are of surpassing importance to her. Suppose finally that *M* does not cherish those ideals and will allow them no scope in any relationship he has with *F*. It makes perfectly good sense here to say that *F* has identified with a passion or desire which is alien to her most significant purposes and concerns and has therefore acted in a way which is foreign to her true self. She has made her own fulfilment that much more difficult (and if the passion has gripped her strongly enough, perhaps impossible) of achievement.

That something is more significant for one's purposes does not mean, as this example makes clear, that it amounts to one's most strongly felt preference. Rather it means that it is more central or important to who one is and what one wants to be. It is very likely that *F*'s friends will see clearly how wrong the relationship is for her. Indeed *F* may very well see this herself, to some extent at least, and on the occasions when she does be in inner turmoil. It is in this sort of way that sense can readily be made of talk of the inner or real self, without necessitating any flirtation with dubious metaphysical entities (cf. Neely 1974: 43; Taylor 1979: 181ff; Penelhum 1979: 315ff).

Basically the same conviction underlies the use made by Gerald Dworkin of the phrase 'authenticity in motivation' (1976: 24f). As Dworkin puts it, in forming second-order desires by means of reflective self-evaluation a person's motivational structure comes to have the stamp of authenticity. (With this compare Frankfurt 1971; Neely 1974; and contrast Watson 1975; Thalberg 1977 and 1978.) Dworkin writes (1976: 25):

> It is the attitude a person takes toward the influences motivating him which determines whether or not they are to be considered 'his'. Does he identify with them, assimilate them to himself, view himself, as the kind of person who wishes to be motivated in these particular ways? If, on the contrary, a man resents his being motivated in certain ways, is alienated from those influences, resents acting in accordance with them, would prefer to be the kind of person who is motivated in different ways, then those influences, even though they may be causally effective, are not viewed as 'his'.

Dworkin (and Frankfurt) seem right (as already indicated) in their insistence on the need for authenticity of motivation if a person is to be autonomous. (The previous chapter argues for this view with the proviso that it not involve running together the reflective self-evaluation manifested in the formation of second-order desires and the process of making one's desires one's own by identifying with them.) The passage also provides a useful corrective to a tendency on the part of some writers (e.g. Neely 1974: 48) to make reflective self-evaluation fundamentally a cognitive matter. Reasons and reasoning obviously do play a role but there are other ways in which a commitment to his (or her) wants may be clarified by and for an individual.

The opinions about their own motivations which people form, even after the most careful introspection, are not always the most reliable indicator of their deepest preferences. Suppose, for instance, a person shows remorse over a failure to perform some action which he (or she) believes he ought to have performed (given that he was not self-reflectively aware of any countervailing want or inclination). Or suppose a person shows an unflagging admiration for the behaviour of others even when he regularly fails to measure up to their standards. In cases of this kind, where we seek to determine a person's real desires, we are apt to give maximum credence to such conative considerations. This is especially so where circumstances arise in a person's life which provide a literally unique opportunity to accomplish some important end. Any failure to capitalise on the opportunity will be an irredeemable failure. In such a case a person's remorsefulness may prove the only serious evidence we have of his true desires.

Remorse, unlike guilt feelings or feelings of regret, is a peculiarly appropriate response to a failure to act as one believes one ought, because it is linked with a wish that one had not done what one did. There are also cases where the agent simply cannot sum his (or her) reasons in such a way as to dictate how he should behave because the matter involves desires about which he is deeply ambivalent (Greenspan 1980: sections III–IV). Given such considerations, it appears reasonable to think of the formation of second-order (and, though they are probably uncommon, even higher-order) desires as *indicators* of a person's deepest preferences and ultimately of what desires are identified with. This is compatible with thinking that there are other indicators which can also satisfactorily be taken as supporting a claim that a particular individual does identify with certain of his desires.

There seem then to be no grounds for the disquiet that often arises from discussion of the 'real self'. But there is none the less one excess that is better avoided. It is sometimes true (as Penelhum has reminded us) that a desire or passion which an individual recognises to be dangerous, destructive of himself or even diabolical, may none the less constitute an ingrained, integral part of his nature — so much so that it has to be thought of as part of his real self. But because elements of the self are real, it does not follow, contrary to some popular usage, that they are 'higher'. Better, therefore, to avoid talk of a *higher* self in this context altogether.

II

The failure to identify with a motivational structure which exemplifies the conception one has of one's life is central to an understanding of various important inner obstacles to autonomous existence. These obstacles range through from those neuroses which may give rise to long-term and even permanent incursions into a person's autonomy, to self-deception, to ambivalence, to the kind of anomie produced by an individual's having ill-defined principles of action and on to weakness of will where the effects on autonomy are generally more isolated both in duration and impact. It would be satisfying, not to say neat, if these and other conditions of the inner self that obstruct autonomy could be traced to a single failure in the agent (such as failure of self-awareness). But this seems unlikely if only because, with phenomena like weakness of will and ambivalence, it is not typically the case that failure of action results from a lack of self-awareness.

True, self-knowledge may have a contribution to make to enhancing autonomy: it may enable the agent to avoid situations where his (or her) weakness is apt to be his undoing or to determine which of the contrary values generating his ambivalence will best promote his autonomy, either occurrently or dispositionally. More importantly, even if no unified theory involving reference to a failure of self-awareness will do, it may yet be that until persons achieve awareness concerning their motivations, autonomy, to that extent, will not be exercisable by them. In fact, progress in overcoming neurosis, self-deception and anomie does depend on the achievement of self-awareness about motivation. And a common-sense understanding of the phenomenon commonly (but as Rorty 1980 points out, not always happily) referred to as 'weakness of will' can be defended against philosophical attack and can be illuminated by reference to the agent's failure to identify with motivations that would enhance his most significant concerns and goals.

The neurotic behaves in a self-defeating manner, yet he (or she) can neither account for, nor control, the way in which he behaves. In his later writings, Freud took the view that the neurotic manages to avoid satisfying those instinctual demands or impulses which would generate anxiety by resort to defence mechanisms such as repression despite all the while being unconscious of what is happening. Since such behaviour has a point, indeed can be seen to make systematic sense (in staving off anxiety), the neurotic is often characterised as having unconscious intentions. Provided a suitably restrained reading of such a term is given it does not mislead to speak in this way (Mischel 1970). There are fairly obvious connections between this influential way of thinking about the neurotic's attempt to cope with anxiety-producing impulses and what holds true of the self-deceived person (cp. Fingarette 1969; Hamlyn 1971). Mischel has put the connection neatly (1970: 235):

> . . . the neurotic has avoided the conflict by deceiving himself: his lack of awareness is motivated, he has made himself unconscious of an incompatible impulse which he knows, in one sense of that term, to be his. And he can do that only in so far as he can also keep himself unconscious of the technique he is intentionally using to deceive himself.

With both conditions the role of ignorance as to one's own motivation is of paramount importance. Indeed, if a person were to set out deliberately to deceive himself, the successful achievement of his aim would be hidden from him! This is because the self-deceiver sustains himself in his self-deception by manipulating the evidence in accordance with the personal stake he has in clinging obstinately to a false belief or in giving up a true but displeasing belief for a false but attractive one. Sometimes to bring about such a condition in oneself serves a protective or defensive role as, for example, when a person clings to a belief about whether a loved one involved in an overseas aeroplane crash remains alive despite the fact that the evidence is best read to the contrary (Szabados 1974 and 1974a). Nevertheless, the self-deceived person, in placing a distorted construction on the total evidence, believes what he believes to be true *and* wants what he believes to be true. And this is the means to overcoming a conflict in his beliefs even though he is not aware that it is such a means.

Self-deception, like neurosis, is something from which any person who aspires to exercise autonomy would prefer to be free. The self-deceiver and the neurotic both lack understanding of their own lives or of a part of their lives. What is more, the normal means open to someone for coming to understand his (or her) situation — reflecting on the reasons for his behaviour — is typically ineffective. This is not to say that the person may not know that something is seriously amiss. Neurotics in particular often seek help because they do have some such awareness. With the self-deceived person, the evidence needs to be presented (either by someone else or, eventually, perhaps, by the agent) in such a way that there can be no room for argument, or so that the complexion placed on the evidence can realistically be of only one sort. The toehold in the evidence which provided the person with enough support to distort and misconstrue it and thus reduce its impact on him (or her) has to be shown to be inadequate to the task. It is precisely because the distortion and misconstruction take place beyond the agent's conscious scrutiny that a preliminary to the overcoming of self-deception is a raising of the agent's consciousness. To put it another way, he has to understand how he has imposed an unnatural interpretation on the total evidence.

With the neurotic person, the matter rarely proves so straightforward. The neurotic's awareness of his resort to unconscious defences to avoid facing up to situations is apt to produce anxiety. There probably are cases where a neurosis is in a sense just outgrown — such as that, previously cited, where the neurotic's fear of not being liked disappears upon involvement in a serious loving relationship. In such cases, self-awareness need not be a prerequisite to overcoming inner obstacles to autonomy. Generally, though, the neurotic's self-deceptive defences have more deep-seated origins; they play a critical role in the maintenance of personal stability, however precarious; so much so that considerable effort is required to lay them bare. Even treatment promising successful overcoming of the neurosis may encounter resistance (Freud's case of the 'Rat Man'). Such successes as there are in laying bare the foundations of neurotic behaviour, enabling the victim to cope with the impulses which give rise to his anxiety, nevertheless take a similar course to that involved in defeating self-deception.

Since there is a strong tie between sophisticated self-awareness and the securing of a degree of autonomy in a person's pattern of living, for someone to get on top of neurotic forces which hold sway in his (or her) life, some understanding of these forces is required (Hampshire 1965: ch.2). What has been hidden from the agent — his instinctual impulses, his unconscious defensive manoeuvrings to avoid facing these impulses, perhaps even his resistance to the uncovering of these aspects of his being — has to be revealed in such a way that the agent can see the inappropriateness of the behaviour all this produces. Various forms of psychotherapy have been developed to help the neurotic person see his situation for what it is. The point is not that we should take an uncritical attitude to such techniques. But there can be no doubt that sometimes they work and that, when they do, it is partly because they develop self-awareness in the agent. What has been effective because unconscious must be brought to consciousness if there is to be any likelihood of its being stopped. Where the agent actively participates in the reshaping of his cognitive and affective structures he can identify with the changed or renewed self as continuous with, though different from, his neurotic self.

To get to know a flaw is not to eliminate it. To get the neurotic to understand or become aware of his own psychological processes is not to overcome them. For the neurotic does not merely fail to understand such processes, he also does not control them. The more bound up with a person's self-image the neurosis happens to be, the greater the effort of will that must be made to get beyond self-awareness to self-directedness. Just as the seriously self-deceived person cannot be brought to take the evidence (whatever it may be) at face value, autonomy may on occasion be forsaken, not because of the dynamics of the unconscious, but for the want of the courage, honesty or effort of will by a person to forge his (or her) life into a life of his own.

III

While the effects on an individual's autonomy of his (or her) holding his values in a compliantly second-hand way are readily acknowledged, the effects on autonomy of a lack in inner coherence among an individual's concerns are less often noted. The concern here is not with those cases where the development of new goals interferes with the completion of earlier ones. In cases of this sort what is signified is an altered conception of the individual's life-plan, but that is not incompatible with its being an autonomous one. The present concern rather is with cases where there is no inner unity because the self is divided over which projects to engage in, or over the order in which to engage in them, and thus has no unified life (even in the fairly weak sense that is bound up with autonomy). The impact may be on generalised orientations — ultimate beliefs, norms or goals — or on relatively specific goals. Thus a person who is free to do some particular action may fail to do it if his wanting to do other less significant actions is allowed to interfere with and ultimately frustrate his pursuit of what he would acknowledge to be more significant and more authentically 'him' (or 'her'). The person in truth identifies with the desire he (or she) sees as more important but lets other, lesser desires get in the way. As emerges later in the discussion of weakness of will, there may, of course, come a point where persistence in such a pattern of behaviour forces a revision in judgement (by, say, an external observer) of the person's priorities. But let us stick with our present quarry, the anomic person (to use Durkheim's term). It sometimes happens that the disarray becomes so serious that the person prefers to be told how to live. Once this stage is reached, autonomy has been given up.

To choose this way is simply to take the line of least resistance and to forsake autonomy and the self-esteem and dignity that go with it. So, too, to fall back on techniques which involve bodily intrusions or drastic interventions, like psychosurgery and aversion therapy, may, as Gerald Dworkin (1976: 26ff; cf. Murphy 1975: 24f) has pointed out, enable an individual to have institutional care but fail to uphold his (or her) dignity as an individual. Such techniques ought to be resorted to, therefore, only where the same effect (expressive and supportive of the individual's dignity) is not otherwise achievable, and only where the subject is in a position to give informed voluntary consent to use of such techniques. (If Murphy is right this will never be so while the subject is an inmate of a 'total institution' like an asylum.) For the anomic person the better way, then, is to seek to understand his (or her) malaise by a means which accords due place to his dignity, and that would only seem possible if he can be brought to recognise for himself what produces the frustrations, resentments or sense of resignation he has about the course of his life. Where this is not within his own province, the means for achieving this can extend from the sympathetic, trusted friend who acts as a 'sounding board', to professional counselling.

Benson (1975) expounds very well the theme of self-knowledge but cautions against thinking that the conscious, reflective and critical capacities of a person are the only means by which integration can be achieved. He instances the case of Raskolnikov in *Crime and Punishment* whose reflective and critical capacities had become corrupt, serving to suppress the real self, a self of which (through a dream) Raskolnikov retained some understanding. We need not consider whether Benson is right to claim that something like the idea of *grace* (understood without its religious associations) is needed to account for cases of this sort. But he is probably correct to hold that the conscious, critical reflection of a person is not the only means to attaining integration for (as with neurosis) there may be means of achieving insight and integration which do not depend on these critical faculties.

Whatever the means used, the aim will be the same: to enable the person to gain awareness of his (or her) inner conflicts and to go on to replace the disorder with a realistic hierarchical ordering that reflects the priorities with which he wishes to identify. The test for determining how successfully this latter condition has been satisfied will be the extent of relief from bitterness, frustration and resentment. It would seem foolish to require complete contentment since even given a high degree of autonomy one may none the less regret that certain projects are beyond one's capacity or demand as a prerequisite things to which one is not entitled and so on. But relatively greater contentment there must be if anomie is to be brought under control and the end-state to be one which upholds individual integrity, or, at least, a greater measure of it.

IV

An individual who fails intentionally to do an action which he believes he ought to do, and which is psychologically and physically within his power, need not thereby fail of autonomy (especially in the occurrent sense). But where such a failure has some bearing on the person's broad conception of his life's direction, or where the failure becomes persistent, there will almost certainly be a diminution of dispositional autonomy. Such failures are matters of everyday observation and, sadly, of personal experience. Various philosophers of note, in particular Socrates, Aristotle and Hare (Mortimore 1971), have, however, argued that, for a free agent, there can be no hiatus between belief and action. It is not possible here fully to traverse the issue of 'weakness of will'. But at least enough must be done to dispel the suggestion that it is radically unlike the other inner impediments to autonomy, in that it is either incoherent or incompatible with acting freely or autonomously.

It is sometimes contended that, in agreeing with certain judgements about what we or others ought to do, we imply that we shall act in accordance with those judgements where we are able. In order to assess the force of this contention, it is necessary to determine what criteria have to be satisfied before we are willing to say of someone that he (or she) believes he ought to perform some specified action. Were we able to state a set of criteria sufficient for the truth of the proposition that a person, S, believes he ought to do x, then the conjunction of the assertion that the criteria are actually satisfied with the denial that S believes he ought to do x, would involve something like self-contradiction.

Can a convincing set of such criteria be stated? According to the position set out above, if we suppose S believes that he ought to do x and, moreover, has no wants or inclinations that run counter to his belief that he ought to do x, then we must assert that there is an analytic connection between a statement about his belief and one about his doing action x. Such a view is not without initial plausibility. We do discount the protestations of those who never get around to acting on their well-voiced 'beliefs'. Nevertheless, if this position were correct (i.e. the position that there is no difference between believing one ought to do x and doing x) the only facts which could provide logically adequate grounds for ascribing to S the belief that he ought to do x when he fails to do x, would be ones about countervailing wants or inclinations. But there may be other facts, in particular facts about S himself, which justify the ascription to S of the appropriate belief, despite the failure of S to enact it. Thus where a person shows remorse over his failure (or persistent failures) to do what he claims he ought to do, or where he shows genuine admiration for the behaviour of others and does not flag in his admiration even when he fails to measure up to his professed standards, we do generally ascribe the appropriate beliefs and desires to him.

Still it may be rejoined that we cannot even identify a person's reaction as one of remorse without being satisfied that he (or she) genuinely tries to make amends and to alter his future conduct. The answer is that while remorse is certainly often accompanied by the intention to mend one's ways (and subsequently by the accomplishment of this task) it does not seem that it must be (cf. Rorty 1980a: 498ff). Remorse is the appropriate response (as against feelings of guilt or regret) to a failure to act as one believed one ought, because it goes hand in hand with a wish that one had not done what one did. Moreover, where a person's failure comes in response to a literally unique opportunity, the evidence of remorse (following on the weak behaviour), which is all the relevant evidence we have, is surely sufficient to justify the claim that the person did believe that he ought to have done what he failed to do.

The recognition of the irrevocability of the past is what occasions remorse, since this emotion cannot adequately be characterised without reference to the seeming inability of the agent to restore the situation to what it was prior to acting. For this reason, some writers, like Nietzsche, have concluded that remorse is futile. Others have noted that the remorseful person may also succumb to feelings of utter hopelessness just because the opportunity to restore the situation has been irretrievably lost. The say-so of such writers is, however, not enough to establish that remorse is an unhealthy emotion. On the contrary, it is importantly connected with the sense of caring, which is fundamental to the moral life. We may conclude — even supposing that a person believes he ought to do some act and has no countervailing wants or inclinations — that no analytic connection is established between a statement about the agent's beliefs about what he ought to do and a statement about his doing it. Furthermore, the alleged relation cannot just be weakened to an empirical or probabilistic sort (e.g. that he will do it nine times out of ten) because we are supposed to be looking for a set of criteria *sufficient* for the truth of the doxastic proposition.

Arguing for a necessary connection between a value judgement and action in accordance with it is not the only way in which philosophers have sought to rule out cases of weakness of will. It has also been maintained that since 'believing one ought to do x' implies 'wanting-to-do-x-in-preference-to-anything-else' there is no room for weakness of will of the sort characterised above. Donald Davidson (1969: 95; cf. N. Cooper 1971) has argued that the following principle is self-evidently true:

> If an agent judges that it would be better to do x, than to do y, then he wants to do x more than he wants to do y.

Davidson thinks that a further principle is also self-evidently true, viz:

> If an agent want to do x more than he wants to do y, and he believes himself to be free to do either x or y, then he will intentionally do x if he does either x or y intentionally.

If we take these principles to be conjointly true it appears impossible that an agent should, while uncompelled, intentionally act contrary to his (or her) best judgement.

What Davidson has done is to fuse together valuing and wanting. In order to see how we can consistently resist his conclusion that weakness of will is impossible it is necessary briefly to consider how he achieves this fusing together. For Davidson *any* desire will be appropriately expressed in the form of a value judgement. Normally, of course, value judgements express the verdicts of morality (roughly, concerning the interests of all) and of prudence (roughly, concerning our own long-term interests), as well as mere desires of the moment. A further aspect of Davidson's position is that since intentional, non-compulsive action requires consciousness of what one is doing and causation by a desire, to be rational is just to act in accordance with such a desire. Accordingly, for an agent to do an action when he (or she) believes it would be better, all things considered, to do another thing, is irrational (cf. also Davidson 1982).

Davidson's views on value judgements are, however, too accommodating. We may, therefore, resist his argument against the possibility of weakness of the will. Value judgements based on the interests of others or on one's own long-term interests (or even preferences) can be genuinely accepted, yet violated on occasion because the agent accedes to the pull of immediate preference. If so then an agent may judge that it would be better morally to do *x* than to do *y* and yet want to do *y* more than he (or she) wants to do *x*. This is less deniable than Davidson's account of the nature of valuing. Equally in the case of prudential principles there seem to be no grounds for denying in a non-question-begging way that there can be conflicts between a preference for some immediate pleasure and a preference for a longer-term benefit. The experience of most of us is that we are often ambivalent about what we want and thus any suggestion that we are motivationally of a piece is implausible. We may reasonably conclude that the weak agent is not just irrational. (For fuller discussion of the issue see Pears 1984, esp. chs. 9, 10.)

Many have denied that an agent who acts weak-willedly can be a free (or autonomous) agent. This is a long-standing charge but we shall attend only to the version of it in a recent illuminating paper by Gary Watson (1977). He has argued that if a sufficient condition of compulsive motivation is that the motivation be contrary to the agent's better practical judgement, then weakness of will is a species of compulsion. And if, as seems to be so, compulsive behaviour is unfree, weak behaviour is too. According to Watson, the way to escape this unhappy conclusion is by holding that the weak agent gives in to desires which the possession of the normal degree of self-control would enable him to resist whereas compulsive desires are such that the normal capacities of resistance are or would be insufficient to enable the agent to resist. We can thus avoid collapsing weakness into compulsion by holding that those who are weak fall short of standards of 'reasonable' or 'normal' self-control, whereas compulsives are motivated by desires which they could not resist even if they measured up to normal standards.

Watson goes on to argue that his account has the advantage over the common-sense view in that his can explain weakness (as culpable failure to develop or maintain the relevant capacities of self-control), whereas the common-sense view cannot: it proves insufficient to appeal either to the agent's choice to resist or to the agent's failure to put out enough effort. For Watson, neither appeal to choice nor to a failure to put out sufficient effort can restore the fortunes of the common-sense view. Appeal to choice will not do because the capacity of self-control is special in involving the capacity to counteract and resist the strength of desires which run counter to what one has judged it is best to do. Appeal to a failure in output of effort will not do either, because given the weak agent's strong motive for making an effort, namely his (or her) considered practical judgement, we should conclude in the absence of a special explanation for his not making it (like not thinking the project worth the effort) that he could not resist.

This latest attack on the common-sense view is an impressive one, but an adequate response can be offered. To begin with, weakness of will is not only manifested in failures to measure up to normal standards of self-control. Consider the position of a person of high moral standing who usually resists a degree of temptation which it is beyond the capacity of most ('normal') humans to resist. Suppose that, on some occasion or occasions this person succumbs knowingly to such a temptation. Why should we conclude that he has acted compulsively? To move immediately to such a conclusion is question-begging, for if we suppose that there are no defeating or disabling conditions present, his past resistance gives us warrant to regard him as autonomous here, too. What can be taken as compulsive behaviour in *most* people need not be taken as such for *all* people (cf. Audi 1979: 186f, 190).

Secondly, Watson (1977: 327, 336) mounts his attack from the perspective of a doctrine that we have found cause to reject. He argues rather behaviouristically that it is from an agent's performance of an action that we should infer what his real motivations and convictions are. But, as already argued, there can be indicators (other than doing an action) of a person's true motivations and convictions (as by displaying remorse). On the basis of such arguments, we are entitled to resist Watson's doctrine and the conclusion he draws from it.

The final point we must touch upon concerns Watson's attack on the explanatory power of the common-sense view. Suppose that we have evidence from previous conduct in similar circumstances that a person has the capacity to perform a particular action. Suppose further that it would be implausible to account for his (or her) failure to perform the action on a particular occasion in terms of psychological failure (e.g. a seizing up under pressure). Suppose finally that he fails to do it and evinces deep remorse because he believed he ought to have done the action on the occasion in question. Given all these suppositions, it seems justifiable to conclude that the best explanation of his failure was weakness of will. For he could have done otherwise and it is this capacity which distinguishes him from the compulsive. The coherence of the common-sense view of weakness of will can, therefore, be held on to.

If the conclusion is warranted that weakness of will is a human phenomenon that we do have to reckon with, its impact on autonomy will likewise have to be reckoned with. The degree to which it interferes with a person's autonomy will depend on the seriousness of the actions it affects and on the range of such actions. In general, though, the weak-willed person surely has the advantage over the neurotic or anomic individual whose autonomy may be extensively curtailed. Notwithstanding this, one victory over an individual's 'worst self' may facilitate a breakthrough to greater self-directedness and personal integrity. The role played by self-knowledge or self-awareness, particularly as regards one's capacities and motivation may sometimes prove significant. But self-control will still be needed. As with the inner obstacles considered previously, it is the will which holds the key to their defeat and thus the means to opening the way for the exercise of autonomy.

6 LIMITING AUTONOMY: HARM TO SELF

We now turn to the justifiability of restricting an individual's autonomy to prevent his (or her) adversely affecting his *own* interests. This is the province of paternalism.

Paternalism has generally been thought of as coercive or (at the least) forcible interference with a person's liberty of action, interference which is (believed to be) justified on the grounds that it will prevent harm to that person's interests. (This is *contra* Gert and Culver 1976 and 1979, who deny that paternalism must interfere with liberty or involve coercion.) Opposition to paternalistic interference with adults, whether by the state (legal paternalism) or by private (adult) individuals, is usually based on a concern to preserve human autonomy or self-determination. Liberal individualists have been in the vanguard of this opposition to paternalism. The political creed of liberalism was from its inception centrally about the liberty of the individual to pursue his (or her) own desires and beliefs. Liberals opposed paternal models of authority and social relations, models based on the manner of a father's dealings with his children. Each (adult) individual, whose action was seen as having a bearing only on his (or her) own good, was to be left free to pursue his own conception of the good.

The classic statement of this position is Mill's, as enunciated in *On Liberty* (223–4):

> . . . the only purpose for which power can be rightfully exercised over any member of a civilised community, against his will, is to prevent harm to others. His own good, either physical or moral, is not a sufficient warrant. He cannot rightfully be compelled to do or forbear because it will be better for him to do so, because it will make him happier, because, in the opinions of others, to do so would be wise, or even right.

The individualist tradition has made much, then, of the idea that the autonomous individual has the 'right' to make his (or her) own choices no matter how foolish or self-defeating such choices may be. As the passage from *On Liberty* makes clear, the issue is about the good of individuals, both physical *cum* mental, and moral. In fact the debates have, until quite recently, mostly been about protecting individuals from moral harm, and thus about the justifiability of what has come to be known as the enforcement of morality. At least as regards the enforcement of morality, Mill's views have come to prevail (cf. Hart 1963; R. Dworkin 1966).

The opposition of the liberal individualist tradition to paternalism is clear, but the character of the opposition needs to be made more explicit. In reality, the opposition has centred on so-called 'strong' paternalism — intervention to protect or benefit a person, despite that person's informed and voluntary denial of consent to the paternalistic measures proposed. The opponents of strong paternalism have contended that it is incompatible with a commitment to self-determination. Paternalism of a 'weak' kind, by contrast, involves interference where there is (or is believed to be) a defect in the decision-making capacities of the person interfered with, or where it is necessary to ascertain whether the person's behaviour is fully reflective. Weak paternalism is less often pilloried, but is still criticised sometimes for opening the gates to invasive intrusions in all our affairs. Given, however, that most of us are less than fully rational most of the time (Van De Veer 1980), some writers hold that such intrusions are not 'paternalistic' in any interesting sense of the term (Beauchamp 1976; Gert and Culver 1976). The mainstream position, however, is that weak paternalism is justifiable in so far as *consent* to the interference would be forthcoming were the subject's decision-making capacities restored.

What is not always noticed is that this consent requirement is ambiguous and admits of two readings. First, it may be a counterfactual which applies to a person when his (or her) liberty is restricted. Thus we might ask: if *S* were without defects in his decision-making capacities, would he none the less choose to perform the act now paternalistically being restricted? If the answer is 'no', the weak paternalist would think the paternalistic intervention justified; if 'yes', he would not think it justified. Second, we might construe the consent requirement as restricting justifiable paternalistic interferences to those occasions where the person whose liberty we restrict is suffering from defects in his capacity to make decisions, but who, if these defects were subsequently to be removed, would *at that time* give retroactive approval to our paternalistic actions. The first reading, which gives precedence to the individual's state of mind at the time when he (or she) is paternalistically restrained (after making due allowance for his impaired capacities), is the one that perhaps best captures the intentions of weak paternalists. But the second reading has figured in the thinking af at least some weak paternalists (cf., for example, Woodward 1982: 70f) and is thought by some to be especially promising in relation to justifying various paternalistic interferences with *children*. The fact that subsequent consent would be one sort of evidence to support the counterfactual judgement involved in the former reading may have helped obscure the differences between the two readings.

The nub of the weak paternalist's reasoning is that there is nothing improper about restricting people's self-determination to prevent them from acting in ways to which they neither can occurrently give voluntary consent nor would give consent when fully competent. As well, though, many writers who are staunch opponents of strong paternalism have sought to justify weak paternalism on the ground that it may *enhance* autonomy. Mill, for instance, in discussing why autonomous adults should not be permitted freely to sell themselves into perpetual slavery offers as his reason that it is not freedom to be permitted to give up one's freedom, rather than, for example, suggesting that the person would subsequently consent to the intervention (*On Liberty*, 299–300).

The problem with weak paternalism, taken on its own, is that it fails to do justice to certain widely shared and deeply entrenched moral convictions relevant to paternalistic intervention. This deficiency can none the less be remedied because these convictions do line up well with a policy of (selective) strong paternalism. To support weak, while opposing strong, paternalism is untenable in view of the fact that strong paternalism is sometimes needed to preserve autonomy. Those who seriously value autonomy cannot remain content with weak paternalism.

I

Weak paternalism involves interference with a person's autonomy where there is (or is believed to be) a defect in the decision-making capacities of the person interfered with. Interference is claimed to be justifiable in so far as consent to it would be forthcoming were the capacities in question to be restored. Moreover, some advocates of weak paternalism claim (as reported earlier) that there is nothing improper about restricting people's self-determination, where the object is to prevent them from acting in ways to which they cannot occurrently give genuine consent because their decision-making capacities are impaired. This is legitimate provided only that, had they not been thus affected, they would have chosen differently, or alternatively that they would later have ratified the intervention, given the opportunity. (The idea of subsequent consent faces various difficulties, most of which are ignored when the idea is criticised below. But see Van De Veer 1979a; Husak 1981; Woodward 1982.)

Mill, while holding that (in self-regarding matters) the individual's independence is 'of right, absolute', argues — on the grounds of a defect in their decision-making capacities — that children and those 'in their nonage' fail to possess such an absolute right (*On Liberty*, 224). A similar justification would appear to be in his mind when he sanctions interferences with those who are 'delirious or in some state of excitement or absorption incompatible with the full use of the reflecting faculty' (*On Liberty*, 294). However, in *Principles of Political Economy* (803, 938) Mill allows paternalistic interference where a person is a poor judge or guardian of his or her real interests, especially in matters of education and culture, or where an irrevocable decision has been taken which would have far-reaching consequences on the distant, and hence less vivid, interests of the decision-taker. These qualifications, in effect, pick out persons thought *incompetent* to give full-blooded consent in certain matters or make decisions of certain types — decisions 'of certain types' because people are rarely, if ever, incompetent across the board (cf. Murphy 1974: 467f). Other weak paternalists have extended the categories of incompetence to include the senile, the mentally ill or handicapped, the compulsive and the ignorant on the ground that these, too, are persons whose capacity to choose in ways that promote their welfare or satisfy their needs is defective. (For further discussion see Brock 1980 and, in more critical vein, Sartorius 1980.)

Armed with a better appreciation of the range of conditions under which weak paternalistic interventions are thought to be appropriate, we now turn our attention to the idea of actual or anticipated consent. It is this consent which is claimed to nullify the otherwise objectionable features of paternalism.

Certainly *actual* consent may mandate paternalism, as in Dworkin's example of Odysseus who ordered his underlings to restrain him in the presence of the Sirens (G. Dworkin 1972: 77). (What happens when such consent is withdrawn is a question to which weak paternalists have given no direct answer.) Most of the incompetents mentioned by weak paternalists are held to be justifiably restricted on the grounds that they would have chosen differently had they been more favourably placed in regard to the qualities and capacities needful for making informed, voluntary choices. Support for this claim conventionally takes the form of a presumption that people who allow themselves to be injured or harmed are, in doing so, not consenting freely and knowingly. Thus Mill remarks of the person (justifiably) restrained from crossing an unsafe bridge that he will come to appreciate the restraint because 'liberty consists in doing what one desires, and he does not desire to fall into the river' (*On*

Liberty, 294; cf. Ten 1971: 65; 1980: 109). In similar vein, Dworkin sees the paternalistic treatment of adults as regards their health and life as a kind of insurance policy taken out against making decisions which are far-reaching, potentially dangerous and irreversible. (Compare also Murphy 1974: 481 who, *à la* Rawls, sees limited paternalism as justifiable in the absence of a guarantee that individuals not be reduced to such incompetence as would compromise their access to primary goods.)

But what of the notion of *anticipated* consent? Rosemary Carter (1977) has pointed out that, especially with children, subsequent consent can be achieved by manipulation (of beliefs or preferences or of relevant information). A child, subject to the successful distortion of beliefs, desires and preferences, might come to approve of the pressures used to develop precisely those beliefs and attitudes. Such consent hardly justifies the earlier interference. Similar considerations would apply to an adult who is made the subject of manipulation (or, a more extreme case, who is 'brainwashed' into a new set of beliefs) and comes thereby to approve of the manipulation, or the brainwashing (cf. Rawls 1971: 249f).

In the absence of a theory of distortion, Carter's principle is not as helpful as may at first appear. Whether we acknowledge distortion or not tends to turn on what we *value*. This may circularly lead us to apply our conception of the good for a person as a criterion for the proper objects of rational and informed consent. Compare Carter's case of parents from a narrow religious sect (who distort the development of their child's intellectual or artistic skills) with the quite different example of a man brought up to see his future in industry and commerce, and who finds this world exciting and competitive and who, accordingly, sees himself indebted to his parents for preparing him to enter the world he relishes (cf. Kleinig 1983: 61ff). It should perhaps be granted that, if some theory of psychological distortion and manipulation were to be developed (taking away the necessity to rely on the 'pre-theoretic intuitions' to which Carter appeals) it might be possible to establish where consent had been manipulated and to reject paternalism allegedly justified by way of such 'consent'. This would be so even where the beliefs, preferences and so on that were shown to have been manipulated were right or good.

Clearly no acceptable theory of psychological distortion is ready to hand, but it does not seem unreasonable to anticipate that one will ultimately be developed. So rather than pursue the objection raised against the weak paternalist's 'anticipated consent' on the grounds of circularity, it may be better to consider a difficulty which is less likely to prove so tractable. This more serious difficulty concerns the implications for the weak paternalist approach when there is good reason to believe some individual would not subsequently thank us for interfering (and so, other things being equal, would not have consented either at the time or afterwards to the intervention). The rebuttable presumption on which the anticipated consent model is built may, in other words, be rebutted and so fail to hold in particular cases since it relies on what is at best a strongly supported empirical generalisation.

Suppose a child never comes to agree that the fluoride tablets administered by his or her parents were worth it. Suppose a person, even after lengthy discussion of his (or her) intention, does not appreciate our stopping him from jumping off a high bridge, or from swimming after dark on an unpatrolled beach known to have dangerous riptides. We cannot properly infer the irrationality of such people merely because they wish to jump or swim in such circumstances. But the screws can be turned still harder against the alleged sufficiency of weak paternalism: suppose *S* knows that heroin addiction causes severe physical harm and likely death before 30 years of age, but still chooses to take the drug because he wants the pleasure of the moment more than anything else. Assume, furthermore, that we independently have good grounds for believing *S* is emotionally stable and of sound reason. A policy of weak paternalism cannot in such a case justify intervention to prevent *S*'s taking heroin. A strong paternalist, as we shall see, would argue for intervention where the consequence of *S*'s action would be to undermine other more dispositional commitments.

It is instructive to consider first what weak paternalists have said of these problematic cases for their position. Carter's position is quite clear. She bites the bullet and contends that, if the motive for legislating against heroin usage is to prevent people harming themselves, such legislation will be unjustified. But she none the less suggests (1977: 145) that if a majority of citizens want the legislation as a safeguard against their own weakness of will (and at the same time require a *sacrifice* on the part of those who do not want such legislation) the legislation will be paternalistic and justified. The strong impression given is that this accounts for why we do endorse interventionist policies on the taking of heroin. Carter's claim appears to represent an *ad hoc* manoeuvre to save a theory.

More importantly, Carter's reasoning is unconvincing when applied to the restrictions placed on professional boxing between grossly ill-matched boxers, or contracting to become a wage-slave, ritual human sacrifice of consenting participants from weird cults, voluntary participation in unnecessary, risky experiments, minimum wages and conditions, pyramid selling and so forth. Nor are the restrictions imposed in these cases plausibly to be accounted for in non-paternalistic terms. We may conclude that the weak paternalist position is at odds with widely held and deeply entrenched moral convictions to the effect that either the state or other adults are justified in intervening in just such cases. Of course, a weak paternalist of Carter's persuasion might contend that, if such paternalistic convictions are so deeply entrenched, we must take the radical step of jettisoning them. But even in a period where the clamour for liberty rights is at a peak, there appears to be little or no weakening in the support for (strong) paternalist interventions *in matters like those listed*. Rather than conclude that it is these convictions that are benighted, and hence to be spurned, the better course is to give up an exclusivist weak paternalism. This is especially so in view of the consideration that the concern for autonomy reflected in support for weak paternalism can also be protected under a policy of (selective) strong paternalism with careful guidelines.

Let us turn to Dworkin. Whether Dworkin is accurately to be regarded as a weak paternalist is open to dispute. At least two writers (Bayles 1974; Hodson 1977) take Dworkin to be defending a strong form of paternalism. Unfortunately, what Dworkin says provides conflicting evidence (as he has acknowledged in his 1983). He frequently emphasises the importance of future-oriented consent and this, as we have seen, is characteristic of weak paternalists. He also writes about restricting a person's voluntary actions whenever it can reasonably be claimed that *fully rational* persons would choose such restrictions, from which it may be inferred that the individual's actual choices need not prove decisive (presumably because they are not to be thought of as fully rational). The issue is not cleared up when we attend to the instances of justified paternalism he offers. In the main they involve impaired choices (e.g. taking addictive drugs which hinder reasoned choices or attempting suicide while under psychological pressure), but there is one apparently clear exception. It comes in the course of his exposition of Mill's views on slavery where he appears to agree with Mill that paternalism is justifiable even when a decision to become a slave is voluntarily taken (G. Dworkin 1972: 75f).

Despite what he says on this last-mentioned matter the general drift of Dworkin's essay (particularly in section VI) and the balance of the evidence presented suggests he is appropriately thought of as a weak paternalist. His discussion of what fully rational individuals would (hypothetically) agree to in the way of paternalistic restrictions is best read as evidence that he thinks it sometimes prudent to restrict our liberties because we do not always occurrently recognise what is in our best interests, in the way that fully competent individuals would do (1972: 78).

With the preliminaries behind us, we can now turn to his discussion of the hard cases for weak paternalism.

Dworkin offers as examples of distinct sorts of irrationality the Christian Scientist — in fact he should have said Jehovah's Witness — who prefers to die rather than have a blood transfusion and the person who, while aware of the risks, refuses to wear a seat-belt in an automobile because of the inconvenience. The second person will, according to Dworkin, be shown just to have miscalculated if he (or she) is like most people, except that he places an enormously high negative value on inconvenience. The Jehovah's Witness, by contrast, attaches incorrect weights to certain of his values. Dworkin thinks that, where evaluative differences are involved, there should be greater reluctance to act paternalistically. He, accordingly, would support intervention in the second, though not the first, of his cases.

There are two points to be made. First, Dworkin relies on our accepting that the person who refuses to wear a seat-belt solely because of its inconvenience would be open to persuasion once the calculations of risks are laid before him (or her). But it would only be 'irrational' of a person to refuse to be swayed by the calculations in the sense of *irrationality* which does duty for *incorrectness*. To say of a person in the case where he fails to do the calculations correctly that he is irrational is only to say that he is objectively wrong about the matter in question. This forces us beyond the sense of 'rationality' appealed to in the weak paternalist case. It also suggests that Dworkin has overlooked cases where people are not ignorant but instead simply fail to care for their interests in the proper way.

Second, those who support intervention in such a case as that of the Jehovah's Witness do so on the grounds that such a person is also wrong to think as he does. He is to be regarded as evaluatively deluded. There is a parallel evaluative delusion in the case of selling oneself into slavery. (Not for nothing is there a famous work, *Thirty Years a Watchtower Slave*, by a Jehovah's Witness who was liberated from the organisation.) Yet Dworkin's judgement suggests otherwise. Hence if his earlier remarks on slavery are tantamount to an endorsement of strong paternalism, he is here inconsistent. Better, perhaps, to see the weight of evidence on the side of his being a weak paternalist, while, like Mill, adopting a position on voluntary slavery which sits uneasily with the weak paternalist stance. (Richard Arneson (1980) tries to show that Mill's views on paternalism and slavery were just an aberration and so can be dismissed by more consistent weak paternalists. But the seriousness with which other weak paternalists like Dworkin and Feinberg have taken the matter suggests otherwise.)

II

The response is sometimes made to criticisms like those advanced in the previous section that they have plausibility only if we accept not just strong paternalism but the *enforcement of morality* as well. In advocating (legal or other) control or prohibition of certain practices — like slavery, prostitution, and drug-taking — or in lending support to laws designed to require the use by employees of safety equipment in noisy or hazardous places of work or even in requiring workers to contribute to superannuation schemes, the strong paternalist, it is claimed, is advocating that his (or her) own moral values be enforced, even on those who do not share them. In urging the priority of, for example, harm prevention over voluntary participation in harmful activities (like the taking of heroin), does the strong paternalist seek the translation of *his* value commitment into a law for *all*? (Cf. Harris 1977; and Pierce 1975 who criticises Hart 1963, for failing to separate paternalism from the enforcement of morality.)

The strong paternalist might be tempted to respond to the effect that the weak paternalist's position is no more satisfactory because in advocating the priority in law of the standard of voluntariness, the weak paternalist is also seeking legal enforcement of his moral position. Thus all laws that have a paternalistic character invoke moral values. Although tempting, this response is insufficiently broad. The legal moralist is concerned with the protection of persons from 'moral harm', and the young from moral corruption (Devlin 1965: 11f). By contrast, the strong paternalist — even where advocating interference of a kind which compels the citizen's involvement in activity which he (or she) considers immoral (like compelling a Jehovah's Witness to have a blood transfusion) — is not concerned with the protection of persons from a self-imposed moral harm. The interconnectedness of legal and moral matters is not the point at issue in discussion of the enforcement of morality.

It might seem more promising for the strong paternalist simply to borrow from the weak paternalist account of the distinction between paternalism and legal moralism advanced by C.L. Ten (1980: 113ff). Ten points out that (weak) paternalistic intervention is not aimed at preventing moral wickedness (or, if this should appear too strong, 'moral harm'). Second, he notes that the ground for paternalistic intervention is the protection or promotion of the interests of particular persons who are to be prevented from harming themselves. Intervention is thus anchored in specific interests. In contradistinction, the enforcement of morality is justified typically by appeal to various general considerations, like the preservation of shared moral values or a particular set of social institutions (cf. Devlin 1965: 16ff). These considerations may have little or nothing to do with the interests of the persons whose moral behaviour is subject to legal proscription.

While this response is one with which a weak paternalist may be satisfied, it is not one that will do the whole job for the strong paternalist. The latter will preserve Ten's distinction between paternalism and legal moralism. But with one class of cases, the question whether we most appropriately talk of strong paternalism, or of the enforcement of a moral position, becomes a moot point. The attendant risk is that of associating strong paternalism with the odium that surrounds talk of the enforcement of morality.

Consider again the case (which we have seen proves troublesome to weak paternalism) of permitting a person freely and knowingly to contract into slavery. Mill, for instance, claims that giving due recognition to the principle of individual freedom cannot require that a person should be free not to be free. It is, he says, not freedom to be allowed to alienate one's freedom. This is all, of course, utterly *a priori*, since there are various considerations which might induce a person freely and knowingly to contract into slavery: in return for a great benefit one has received or will receive; for reasons of religious devotion; as a means of advancing some cause of deep importance and so on. Despite the failure of this weak paternalistic line of Mill's, Mill himself gives a clue, if not a well-developed argument, as to how we might justify intervening to prevent people from freely and knowingly selling themselves into slavery (cf. Dworkin 1972: 76). Mill points out in *On Liberty* (299) that to permit people such a liberty would prevent the preservation of their liberty *to make future choices*. As he puts it: '. . . But by selling himself for a slave, he abdicates his liberty; he forgoes any future use of it beyond that single act . . .'

To restrict a person's immediate freedom is sometimes to promote a wider range of future freedoms for the person. Here is the link with autonomy. To be autonomous is to be one's own man or woman; it is not merely to be free but to be free to order one's life in a unified way according to a plan or conception which fully expresses one's own individual preferences, interests and so on. We need (as stated before) to distinguish the occurrent sense from the dispositional sense of autonomy. When we talk of people acting autonomously in particular situations, we are talking of their occurrent autonomy. But when we wish to make an overall judgement about the self-directedness of someone's life, what is at issue is whether, in the main, it is ordered according to a plan or conception which fully expresses his (or her) own will. The term 'plan', as previously explained, refers to whatever it is that a person wants to do in or with his (or her) life and, therefore, covers career, life-style, dominant concerns and so on. (It is obvious, of course, that people's preferences, interests and so on do not always coincide and as well that an individual's other values may come to assume at some time more importance for him than his autonomy, so the commitment we have to the value of personal autonomy is at best a defeasible commitment.)

Since slavery, no matter how gladly the act of becoming a slave is entered into, renders one human the mere possession or property of another and thereby violates the individual's dispositional autonomy, we are justified in intervening to prevent persons contracting into it. Whether or not such intervention is to be characterised as 'strong paternalism' or as 'the enforcement of a moral position' turns on whether the protection of an individual's liberty to make future choices is in his (or her) interest all things considered. If a person forgoes his dispositional autonomy by contracting voluntarily into permanent slavery and is judged to be *harmed* in consequence (the loss of autonomy more than counterbalancing any gains from enslavement), intervention to stop the enforcement of the contract is strongly paternalistic.

However, if the gains derived from contracting voluntarily into permanent slavery outweigh the loss that stems from forgoing dispositional autonomy, such that it is actually to the *benefit* of the individual to become a perpetual slave, then to prohibit such a contract would not be strongly paternalistic. If such a prohibition is to be justified, it would seem that it must be done on the grounds that it is *immoral* for one person to own another. So where the benefits anticipated by the would-be slave are significant, and not available without enslavement, to intervene to prevent enslavement would be to enforce a moral position. The immorality involved in one individual 'owning' another, however, bears no relation to the standards of sexual morality which Devlin and others urge should be enforced by the state in order to prevent 'moral harm' and even to maintain societal integrity.

Of course, the notion of 'moral harm' is not an altogether clear one. It is perhaps most useful in relation to intervention involving children, rather than adults. For instance, a case might be made for giving custody of a child to his father, despite the child's preference for his mother, if his mother is likely to bring the child up as a Nazi or as a child prostitute. It is, perhaps, because such an upbringing seems likely to be against the child's interest in developing sound moral values that talk of 'moral harm' seems reasonably natural.

Even where we clearly place a high value on autonomy, especially in its dispositional dimension, it is necessary to reiterate that commitment to it remains defeasible. Suppose that the authorities in a certain country have indicated that they will not permit the members of a particular family to emigrate except in exchange for a key member of it who is in exile. Suppose further that, while there is no threat of physical harm to the resident members of the family, the exchange would free them from serious and ongoing harassment. Suppose, finally, that it is known that, if the wanted exile puts himself in the hands of the authorities, he will become a virtual slave to the regime. In this case, intervention would clearly be strongly paternalistic. But despite the high value we place on autonomy, we might refuse to intervene in such a case on the grounds that consequentialist considerations must override (allowing that our scruples about dealing with people corrupt enough to exact such bargains can be set aside). In cases of this sort, consequentialist factors are sufficiently significant to take precedence over such normally prior values as doing justice, protecting such human rights as there may be or, as here, preserving autonomy. These consequentialist considerations will sometimes allow a case to be made for *not* intervening to protect people from voluntarily entering into perpetual enslavement. (As regards renewable slavery contracts, see Ten 1980: 119.)

The conclusion we reach is that a commitment to strong paternalism does not require a parallel commitment to the 'enforcement of morality' (as the latter is understood by Devlin and others). The strong paternalism supportive of autonomy seeks to protect an individual from harming his (or her) own interests, especially as these are reflected in his life-plan. By contrast, the enforcement of morality is intended to defend the individual only from one alleged sort of harm — moral harm — and may even override the interests of the individual where more general interests, such as the upholding of shared moral values, are at stake.

The central point remains, that those who value autonomy highly must also accept strong paternalism — whatever else may be said regarding the relationship between the latter and the enforcement of morality. Moreover, strong paternalism avoids the limitations of its weak counterpart, and so will do the same job, while doing it better.

III

Even if one drops the objection that strong paternalism commits one to having to enforce morality, other objections may seem less easily overcome. Feinberg (1971: 120ff), for instance, has mounted a relevant objection to strong paternalism. He urges that, if we take respect for a person's voluntary choice as such as an ultimate principle, then we can consistently oppose strong paternalism in all its manifestations. Let us see what this comes to with the all-crucial case of voluntarily contracting into perpetual slavery. Feinberg's response to this is to hedge his bets by claiming that administrative considerations, for instance the cumbersome and expensive legal machinery that would be needed to test for voluntariness, justify outlawing such slavery.

There are several comments to be made about his position. First, unless Feinberg is to be read as holding *à la* Nozick that non-violation of autonomy is a side-constraint on actions, acceptance of Feinberg's ultimate principle would commit one to giving precedence to the worth of occurrent autonomy — the choice of the moment — rather than to dispositional autonomy, since enslavement clearly impinges on the whole pattern of a person's choices. It is far from obvious that such a commitment is desirable. Second, in defending his claim about the administrative complications that would be associated with *extreme* forfeitures of freedom, Feinberg points out that certain resignations of liberties are obviously permissible and cites such legally sanctioned practices as foregoing particular liberties in reasonable employment contracts or commercial ventures. Two comments here seem relevant. To begin with, it is not enough to cite such instances of limited, albeit extensive, forfeitures, because one of the grounds on which we differentiate reasonable contracts involving forfeitures from unreasonable ones (amounting to perpetual slavery) is the extent and nature of the curtailed liberties. We can and do want to differentiate such matters — as Feinberg would agree — so it is no help to cite the reasonable forfeitures to underpin a doctrine, even a hedged one, of the sovereignty of the voluntary chooser. As well, though, Feinberg is not persuasive in his contention that the legal machinery that would be needed to test voluntariness in such a way as to warrant our outlawing slavery would be cumbersome and expensive. His contention is not persuasive for the reason that we already find it needful and possible to test voluntariness in other important legal matters, and seem certain to be required to do so in even greater degree if anticipated legal changes occur in relation to, for example, voluntary euthanasia. Even if Feinberg's claims were persuasive, they could hardly provide the whole ground for any *principled* policy that a society might develop in relation to slavery contracts, voluntary taking of heroin or voluntary participation in seriously risky, unnecessary experiments.

Yet, it may still appear that there is something fishy about the claim that a policy of strong paternalism (even a selective one) can be justified on the grounds that it preserves autonomy. Isn't it true that, in paternalistically preventing someone (who wants to) from selling himself (or herself) into perpetual slavery, the strong paternalist is thereby violating that person's autonomy? Indeed, isn't it tantamount to treating the person in question in precisely the way the master treats the slave? Undoubtedly in this challenge is to be found the emotional core of the opposition to strong paternalism.

As indicated previously, in the dispositional or comprehensive sense of autonomy, a person's career, life-style, dominant concerns and the like will be central to his (or her) conception of his life. Autonomy as regards the important interests in a person's life must be dispositional rather than occurrent, because only in the former sense does the course of an individual's life enjoy a unified order and avoid self-defeating conflict in fundamentals. To maximise autonomy over the course of a lifetime, dispositional autonomy must be preserved. If it is this conception of autonomy which we should seek to foster, then strong paternalist interventions will sometimes be needed. The strong paternalist may thereby be required to violate occurrent autonomy but, unlike the weak paternalist, he will think such forfeitures worthwhile because they succour dispositional autonomy.

IV

Even those who thus far accept *in principle* the preceding argument for strong paternalism may none the less be reluctant to support it *in practice*. Some attention needs, therefore, to be given to the guidelines appropriate to the implementation of a policy involving strong paternalism, particularly as regards legal paternalism. We may begin with a claim by Mill (and more recently by Sartorius 1975: 155f) that, even where (legal) paternalism is governed by the best of intentions, it is more often than not misguided.

In *On Liberty* (283) Mill writes:

> But the strongest of all the arguments against the interference of the public with purely personal conduct is that, when it does interfere, the odds are that it interferes wrongly, and in the wrong place. On questions of social morality, of duty to others, the opinion of the

public, that is, of an overruling majority, though often wrong, is likely to be still oftener right; because on such questions they are only required to judge of their own interests; of the manner in which some mode of conduct, if allowed to be practised, would effect (*sic*) themselves. But the opinion of a similar majority, imposed as a law on the minority, on questions of self-regarding conduct, is quite as likely to be wrong as right; for in these cases public opinion means, at the best, some people's opinions of what is good or bad for other people . . .

This is a curious argument though not chiefly for the reason offered by Hart in criticising Mill, namely that we are now less inclined to believe that individuals know their own interests best (Hart 1963: 32f). It is curious rather because it begs the question in supposing judgements (by others) of harm to certain individuals to be matters of mere opinion. Moreover, in the general discussion, as well as in the particular passage, Mill uncharacteristically appears to conflate the enforcing of morality with (weak) paternalism. For instance, Mill gives his famous example of legislation by Muslims against the eating of pork and then concludes his argument by urging that 'The only tenable ground of condemnation would be, that with the personal tastes and self-regarding concerns of individuals the public has no business to interfere' (285). This, by his own admission, is to do with a matter of morality as far as Muslims are concerned, but is diminished here by Mill to a matter of personal taste, even though he began by 'speaking of conduct which, while it does no wrong to others, is supposed to do great harm to the agent himself' (283).

Mill's argument clearly does not provide an absolute barrier to paternalism. But its confusions militate even against his claim that paternalistic legislation would be misguided. Earlier, without reference to mere 'opinion', examples were provided showing that serious harm may still befall individuals despite the fact that their engagement in some specified activity (perhaps heroin taking) is entirely voluntary. As well, one can distill from the writings of two recent defenders of weak paternalism several considerations which go some way to calm such fears as those expressed by Mill regarding the harmful (if unintended) effects of well-motivated paternalism.

Dworkin (1972: 82ff) and Murphy (1974: 483ff) have advanced criteria for limiting the scope of paternalism. Basically, these criteria operate to specify, closely and systematically, the nature of the harm to be prevented. A prominent consideration is whether the harm is of a serious kind and, associated with this, whether it is easily reversed. Grave harms, such as loss of future liberty, erosion of mental powers, and serious physical impairment, can be regarded as direct obstacles either to autonomy or its enjoyment. Thus, where a drug has the effect of causing permanent brain damage, the case for paternalistic prevention of the taking of the drug is radically unlike that for marijuana usage. Similarly, multiple ingredient analgesics causing renal damage to significant numbers of users will be in a different case to single ingredient ones.

A second concern is the extent and character of the intervention to be countenanced. The intervention must clearly be linked to the harm-threatening behaviour; be limited in duration; and, where the paternalism is legal in character, the procedures to be followed and the personnel who are to have the power of interference must be clearly specified.

Thirdly, Dworkin argues that, given 'the resources of ignorance, ill will and stupidity available to the law-makers of a society' (1972: 83), a heavy and clear burden of proof rests on the state to demonstrate the exact nature of the seriously harmful effects (or beneficial consequences) and their probability of occurrence. This would seem especially to be so where the activity at issue plays a determinative role in a person's life-plan as with, say, a war reporter, a racing driver or a mountain climber. Thus, while there might be circumstances where the weather is such that even skilled mountain climbers should be prevented for a time from climbing, one could not normally urge the argument from autonomy as the basis for hindering a person in the pursuit of a life-plan that revolves around the conquest of mountain hazards.

Lastly, and perhaps most important, paternalistic interventions should not be directed at producing a continuing state of dependence, but rather be used to increase the dispositional sovereignty of the agent. They are instruments of last resort.

It may be thought by some readers that the position defended here is obviously faulty where *death* is the harm threatened by a person's behaviour or proposed behaviour, and, thus, indefensible overall. Surely, it may be said, suicide and voluntary euthanasia should not be restricted even under the safeguards just outlined. Are we not in danger of returning to the oppressive *mores* of earlier generations on such matters if strong paternalism is endorsed? The argument from autonomy once again comes into its own here. Those who seek voluntary euthanasia generally do so because they have incurable conditions which involve intolerable pain and suffering, or because, in obtaining relief from such pain, they forfeit a recognisably human existence. Generally speaking, their state of suffering requires them to make their request in advance by way of a 'living will' (Young 1976). Such persons clearly have concluded quite reasonably that the fulfilment of further aspects of their life-plan is now out of the question. Death for them would be a benefit. In acceding to their request for voluntary euthanasia, we preclude no significant future choices. So the appropriateness elsewhere of legal paternalism — whether of the strong or weak variety — need not imply opposition to the legalisation of voluntary euthanasia. In relation to suicide, similar points are in order. Where there is established a clear irrationality about the range and significance of autonomy open to a would-be suicide, an other-things-being-equal appeal on weak paternalist grounds should suffice to justify restraining the individual. Where other things are not equal, as perhaps in a 'protest' suicide, external factors might be seen as overriding. There can, of course, sometimes be non-paternalistic justifications (or not wholly paternalistic ones) for preventing suicides, for instance where harm to others will otherwise be occasioned. The strong paternalist need not, therefore, be committed to a policy which threatens to undermine human freedom over such an important area as death or the manner of one's dying.

Every community must consider whether the *gain* in having legal scope for paternalistic interferences (as well as interpersonal scope) is sufficiently worthwhile to warrant the effort and trouble needed to establish guidelines that will minimise manipulation for the purposes of arbitrary or repressive interferences with liberty (and not merely for adults — see Murphy 1974; Beauchamp 1977; Young 1980b). It is necessary to consider whether there would be any *loss* from failure to provide in law for strong paternalism. The argument put here is that there is a gain to be had which is worth the effort of establishing careful guidelines. Failure to make this provision would, for some people, some of the time, significantly diminish their autonomy as regards primary human goods.

7 LIMITING AUTONOMY: HARM OR OFFENCE TO OTHERS

Autonomy is of fundamental significance for our understanding of moral personhood. In exercising autonomy we shape our own lives, an engagement valuable in itself. There are, however, other goods which sometimes take precedence over autonomy. Although important, autonomy constitutes only one of the elements of the good. Moreover, one individual's autonomous choices and actions may interfere with the exercise of a like autonomy by others. Given the value and importance to an individual of autonomy, it cannot lightly be set aside. But respect for one individual's autonomy cannot require the rest of us to protect it at whatever cost to ourselves.

In view of the conflict that may arise between one individual's autonomy and that of others, the question must be decided as to the proper limits of each person's autonomy. This issue is crucial since failure to set these limits properly can only result in an unjustified diminution in the scope some will have to pursue their own life-plans and purposes (given individual variations in strength and vulnerability).

Aside from exceptional cases like those which arise in certain competitive arenas (e.g. sport), it has traditionally been thought that any exercise of autonomy that results in *harm* or *injury*, or *threatens* unreasonably to do so, entitles the sufferer to protection. Sometimes, though, the autonomous behaviour of one individual occasions not harm but *offence* to some other individual. The tradition here has been less sure, but there has been some support for the claim that the offended individual is also entitled to protection. If we suppose for the moment that there is a case in each of these kinds of circumstance for affording such protection, it seems fairly obvious that this will require limiting the autonomy of one (or some) of the individuals involved. So, supposing still that a supporting case can be mounted, it looks to be legitimate *on occasion* to restrict one person's autonomy so as to secure another person's interests. (Needless to say it is not just *autonomous* actions which are capable of putting the interests of others at risk in these ways.) Since such restrictions will have the character of impositions, they will involve compulsion or coercion.

I

Autonomy is valued at least in part because it is a means to the fulfilment of wants (see Chapter 3). If the autonomous behaviour of one person, R, causes harm to another person, S, then R seriously interferes with the fulfilment of S's wants and, other things being equal, that is a bad thing. If R assaults S, there can be no doubt that S has been wronged. R has interfered with S's capacity to satisfy his (or her) wants, which is (other things being equal) injurious to S's interests. To have an interest in something is to have a stake in it such that one stands to gain or lose depending on the condition or outcome of the thing (Feinberg 1977; Bayles 1978: ch. 5). For present purposes, losses may be thought of as being sustained in connection *either* with the interests people have in matters to do with their welfare (e.g. health) *or* in the achievement of the ulterior goals that reflect what they want to do in and with their lives. The former constitute indispensible means to the latter, but are also constitutive of the person's good, regardless of that person's wants.

It may appear to follow from what has been said that, for an individual to be harmed, he (or she) must be made less able to satisfy his wants. This is not quite accurate. It is not only when a person's interests are damaged by the autonomous actions of another that there is proper cause to restrict the injurer's autonomy, but also (as indicated earlier) when the former's interests are put at unreasonable risk by such autonomous actions. (We may take it as read that, if a person suffers psychologically as a direct result of being exposed to unreasonable risk from another's autonomous activity, his case falls under the head of straightforward damage to interests. This is because we have preferences for, and hence, other things being equal, an interest in, psychological states like contentment and absence of anxiety.)

Many cases of an individual's legitimate interests being jeopardised by the actions of others concern the actions of government instrumentalities or commercial enterprises. There are many contemporary cases where individuals have complained about the location of nuclear power plants and aluminium smelters, the disposal of industrial effluent, the manufacture of unsafe goods and so forth. In order to determine, in cases like these, whether it is morally proper to limit the autonomy of the instrumentality or enterprise for the sake of protecting the autonomy of various individual citizens or consumers, it is necessary to know the likelihood of harm eventuating. A risk can, for instance, be created without posing any serious threat, and even a substantial threat need not be classified as serious, provided the associated harm is sufficiently remote.

If an individual's or entity's activities do pose a serious and immediate threat to the satisfaction of someone else's legitimate interests, the onus of showing why it would not be morally proper to limit the former party's freedom falls on that party. Since these kinds of case typically involve damage to property, or put at risk the life or health of persons the onus is commonly a heavy one. To defend against such risks would almost certainly necessitate legal intervention of one sort or another. (See further, Hart and Honoré 1959; Gross 1979.)

The likelihood of the onus being discharged depends in part upon the goals being pursued by the party generating the risk. This is obviously an important consideration in relation to, for instance, the location of major installations and the mining and manufacture of hazardous substances because the economic effects (e.g. on employment, fuel supplies and so on) of such projects may be of great moment to the wider community.

Often such community-wide benefits will have to be set over against the fact that they are obtained at the risk of damage to the health of workers in the industry or the well-being of those living in the surrounding area. Thus a further consideration to be taken into account is the availability of other avenues for achieving the benefits promised by such a project, without jeopardising the interests others have in maintaining control over their lives, health and property. Just as many a project is defended on the grounds of its importance, so are many opposed on the grounds that less harmful means of implementation are possible.

The principles enunciated have much wider application than this concentration on the activities of large instrumentalities and enterprises may seem to imply. Certain interpersonal matters, like reckless driving, or the possession of hand guns, fall within the framework because they clearly make for serious hazards to others and lack any redeeming value (or, at any rate, sufficient redeeming value).

To this point, cases have been discussed where the autonomous behaviour of a person or quasi-person occasions or threatens agreed harms to another with consequent impact on this other's autonomy. (Concern has been confined to harms done to other humans in order to keep the discussion manageable, not because harms to non-humans are either unimportant or irrelevant to limitations on autonomy. Wanton cruelty to animals, for example, is intolerable and certainly calls for action to limit the autonomy of those who practise it. Just how wide these limitations should be will depend on what attitudes towards animals we are justified in adopting. That, however, is far too big an issue to canvass here.)

While (as indicated) there are additional factors to be taken into account before restricting the autonomy of a party causing or threatening harm, it is not to be supposed that determining whether R harms S is an altogether straightforward task. Frequently it is, but a moment's reflection will bring to mind some 'hard' cases. If R smokes in public transport, can S rightly claim that he, S, a non-smoker, has been harmed? Supposing there to be a fact of the matter (such that there is a genuine harm done and not merely annoyance occasioned), appeal would have to be made to criteria relevant to the adjudication of clashes between the autonomous behaviour of two (or more) individuals. If the fact of the matter is that non-smokers are exposed to a health hazard in such circumstances the imposition on them would seem more significant than the minor intrusion on the autonomy of smokers which would be involved in restricting smoking in public transport. (See further, Lucas (1966: 62–6) who argues that the [private] harm principle is justified *because* it can be drawn upon to settle such disputes and conflicts of interest.)

Two further complicating considerations need more fully to be addressed here and now. First, the harm wrought by an autonomous agent may not befall another individual or individuals. It may take a more 'public' or social form. Second, the famous legal dictum, *volenti non fit injuria* (i.e. voluntary assumption of risk negates any claim to have been injured) has somehow to be accommodated to the harm principle under discussion, since the former would appear to qualify the force of the latter.

If an individual sabotages a city's sewerage system, it is pretty clear that he has occasioned harm which has a public dimension. Often there are reasons for understanding talk of the 'public interest' as simply referring to the separable interests of the individual citizens who make up the society. Notwithstanding this, the point of talking here of 'public harms' is the straightforward one of referring to harms which are not directed as such at the interests of particular individuals, but at the interests of all indivisibly (Rawls 1971: 265ff). Supposing the activities of governments and their agencies in providing citizens with protection against public harms to be desirable, the same grounds will be available for intervening to prevent public harms (or unreasonable risks of public harm) as for the private harms considered previously. The problems about determining just what are the public harms against which societies are entitled to protect themselves will for the most part be like those that arise with determining what are the private harms against which individuals may rightfully be protected. But because there is greater difficulty in specifying the nature of the public interest, there will tend to be more 'grey' area as regards what constitutes public harms.

Thus it will be no more controversial to urge that treason, sabotage of the nation's defence installations and so forth be thought of as public harms, than it is to urge that assault, murder and so on are private harms. But to go beyond these relatively simple cases, some specification, even a vague one, of the idea of public harm will be needed. One proposal is to think of public harm as the 'impairment of institutional practices and regularity systems that are in the public interest' (Feinberg 1973: 25). This is a proposal of some worth provided that there is due recognition of the vagueness of 'impairment'.

On this proposal, serious interference with public officials (such as judges, law enforcement officers and public servants) in the performance of their official duties would probably be classified as a public harm. This is not to say that such interference (or even acts of treason, sabotage, divulging of official secrets and the like) can never be *morally* justified. Because they involve public harm, they will normally be illegal and that is our chief concern here (but see Young 1977).

But suppose the police decide to go on strike. Should this count as threatening public harm? In some countries, strikes by public employees are outlawed because they are held to create public harm (or unreasonably to threaten it). Ought all countries to adopt such a stance? Michael Bayles has suggested that the activities of certain public officials (like the police) should be distinguished in this regard from those of others (like teachers). He thinks the difference is that the impairment of the activity of teaching can be made up at another time, and hence compensation can be exacted, whereas impairment of the capacity to prevent private injury during a particular period cannot. So strikes by the police should be prohibited while those of teachers need not (Bayles 1978: 117). While this is an interesting proposal, it is not convincing for the reason that states presumably will, under normal circumstances, have at their disposal other personnel (e.g. in the armed forces) who could perform the relevant functions of the police. Thus there need be no impairment of the functioning of the policing service, at least in the short run. Alternative arrangements would seem manageable on a temporary basis for almost all occupations carried out by public officials. Perhaps the hardest to cover would be skilled surgeons in a system of nationalised health care. So it will be hard to justify outlawing strikes by public employees on the ground that they create public harm, in so far as such harm is generally avoidable — which it probably is. (It is, of course, quite a different question whether, in cases where strikes by public officials are illegal, such strike action is on some occasions morally defensible. Things may have come to such a pass that to strike is in conscience the only remaining option.)

Cases of interference with public officials in the performance of their duties, in which no impairment of significant public institutions or services occurs, will be seen to occasion no public harm, and for this reason may be allowed. Whether allowed or not, it remains necessary to test for impairment in each case. Where impairment occurs (or is threatened) there is a significant public harm (or threat of it) and so a reason will be available for intervening to prevent it.

What are we to make of the complications which the legal maxim *volenti non fit injuria* makes for the private harm principle? Let us begin by mentioning briefly how things stand when there is a competitive aspect to the voluntary involvement. Under conditions of private enterprise, one individual's autonomous business activities may adversely affect another's business interests. From Kant and Mill on, such conflicts of interest have not been thought (by liberal or libertarian commentators, at least) to provide any basis for regulation of such activities. For their part they have held that as long as competition is 'fair', the market will settle clashes of interest. This belief seems best understood as founded on acceptance of the *volenti* maxim. Socialists, of course, have argued for greater interventions, in part because competition is often unfair, in part to reduce 'public harms' like the wastage of scarce resources occasioned by such struggles and the impact of external diseconomies or 'spillover' costs, and in part because the exploitation of 'wage-labourers' essential to private enterprise eats into the autonomy of those labourers. What is interesting about this fundamental disagreement is that each side claims to be upholding the value of individual autonomy in advocating its policy on intervention. The libertarian and the liberal, for example, think it crucial to any conception of autonomy for individuals, that it extend to economic liberty (R. Dworkin 1978: 130ff). The socialist believes that failure to regulate autonomy in the economic sphere will harmfully affect the autonomy of others. For the moment, suffice it to say that the liberal and the conservative (especially the libertarian), seem more committed in these competitive contexts to supporting the *volenti* maxim, so long as no hint of criminality is involved.

What is the position where there is no competitive aspect? There is a long history of legal judgements and discussions of the maxim in which the attempt is made to subsume under public harms those personal harms to which people consent. Thus there is, for instance, the notion that it is against the public interest to permit people to consent to their being injured since they will end up a charge on the public purse or be less able to perform their duties as citizens. Again, one of the strands in the well-known argument for the 'enforcement of morality' by Devlin (1965) is the suggestion that social life and certain of its central institutions would be irreparably damaged if people were allowed to consent to participate in activities thought by the enforcers of morality to be harmful, at least to the morals of the individual. Other arguments for the maxim have been concerned with establishing a presumption of ignorance on the part of anyone who consents to a personal harm, especially a serious one, or with assimilating the law's legitimate concern in such cases to its sometime paternalistic role. A recent paper by John Kleinig (1979) has effectively criticised all of these various attempts to justify *volenti*. While the connections with paternalism are perhaps stronger than Kleinig allows, there is merit in his suggestion that the law is sometimes properly called to intervene where the actions of 'the victim' threaten to diminish his (or her) status as a fully fledged moral agent. This is, as he says, clearest where one person, *M*, foolishly agrees to another, *N*, harming him. This might be true in, for instance, sexual relationships where one party, in the absence of physical coercion, consents to the other's sadism (say because of a desire not to have the relationship put under extra strain).

Just what the, or a, satisfactory rationale for the *volenti* maxim may turn out to be need not be decided now. It need only be agreed that there is some intuitive plausibility in the suggestion that there would be a loss to suffer if the maxim were jettisoned. But there is widespread support for the idea that moral and legal justification exists for preventing individuals from autonomously consenting to serious harms such as amputations, physical or sexual abuse and so on. So an individual's autonomy ought sometimes to be limited if the individual consents to harm being done to him (or her) by another. Whatever the list of the circumstances in which such limitations should properly take place, whatever the rationale of such a list and whatever the boundaries within which it should operate, *volenti* has some force (see Feinberg 1984: 115ff).

II

Discussion to this point has deliberately concentrated on damage to the physical and psychological interests of individuals, and on damage to more public interests, which may arise out of the autonomous *actions* of other agents or institutions. It remains now to direct attention to two further important concerns, *privacy* and *speech*. As well, there is the fact that thus far in the discussion of 'harm', the concept has been construed rather narrowly; we shall in due course comment on the possibility of extending it to incorporate the idea of a 'failure to benefit'.

Privacy can be dealt with relatively briefly. It requires consideration because it is likely to come into conflict with the more active autonomy of movement or observation of other people or, perhaps even more significantly, of institutions and governments. This because the demand for privacy or for its protection is a demand to limit the autonomy of others. None of us, except perhaps the 'peeping Tom', doubts that there should be limits to the freedom of others to observe us in our more intimate moments. There are kinds of information about ourselves which should remain *under our control*. If we choose to tell others, that is our business. Or if we choose a life that essentially involves publicity we voluntarily forego some immunity (for reasons having much to do with the *volenti* maxim — see Williams 1978: 62). Deliberate prying by others, however, is not a defensible use of their autonomy. Charles Fried goes further and argues that unless certain sorts of information remain generally unrevealed some personal relationships will be impossible, namely those involving love, friendship and trust (Fried 1970: ch. 9; cp. Rachels 1975; Reiman 1976: 29–39). But what he claims to be a general truth is at best much weaker than that, for friendship is surely at least possible with one whose life is an 'open book'. Moreover, in less individualistic societies, his claim would be thought to have little or no plausibility.

The concern most of us have to retain some degree of privacy, however, is probably occasioned less by the behaviour of other individuals than by the (potential) intrusiveness of corporations, agencies of the state and so on. Thus the acquisition of information about us such as our financial standing or our political activities by way of inquiries outside our ken is an indefensible violation of privacy. It is important to note that it is not simply having such knowledge about us which violates our privacy but the manner of its acquisition. Phone-tapping, the use of 'bugging' devices, the unauthorised searching of financial records by means of computers and the like need to be restricted. As previously mentioned, many writers have suggested that such activities are today on the increase and thus that there is greater need for vigilance.

Some insightful remarks of Hyman Gross (1971) brings out well the basic objectionableness of such practices. These activities, he suggests, involve using or managing the person for the institution's (or offending person's) own ends, and thus diminish the responsible agency of the person from whom control of information about himself (or herself) is usurped. Even where these ends are themselves desirable (e.g. the reduction of crime) there is good reason to proceed carefully because procedures like phone-tapping threaten the place of autonomy in our conception of a good life and hence should only ever be used as a last resort. Obviously enough, questions of national security or of an individual's personal safety will sometimes assume sufficient importance to override a particular person's claim to privacy. But these will be relatively rare. Moreover, the onus will be on the state or its agencies to establish that a citizen's privacy may justifiably be invaded because to do so is necessary to avoid the threat of serious public or private harm. For the most part a person's interest in controlling access to information about himself (or herself) and his activities is one that should be respected. To exercise that degree of control is an important part of what it is for an individual to pursue his (or her) own life-plan. Provided that the exercise of such control poses no serious threat to the well-being of others it should be respected and supported, even to the extent of limiting the autonomy of others to obtain information to which they have no right to be privy.

III

Not everything that we communicate is intended to be private. Much, perhaps most, of what we communicate is intended to reach a wider audience. Accordingly, freedom of expression means a lot to virtually all human beings and even more to those whose life-plans revolve around speech, writing and other vehicles (such as the various art forms) for the dissemination of ideas. In fact partly because it is such a strong personal interest the presumption in its favour is commonly held to be greater than for other freedoms. As well, of course, it is basic to much that is of public significance. Yet it is plain that not just anything should be allowed in speech, in print, on the screen and so forth. Defamation, libel and slander are hardly the kind of things which should be allowed without restriction. Again, given my argument in the preceding section about the protection of privacy, the publication of material about a person without that person's having given access is, other things being equal, surely something to be prevented. Further, the publication of information that would seriously endanger the lives of others (e.g. strategic material in war situations, or the 'recipes' for the manufacture of lethal weapons like personnel bombs and substances like nerve gas) is hardly the kind of activity that should in general be permitted to go on uncensored.

Are we then simply confronted with the task of determining those instances in which untrammelled expression would be harmful? In the formal sense that is perhaps so though there are matters falling under the rubric of free speech (like parliamentary privilege and contempt of court) which cannot be discussed here but which cast doubt on any such

simplification. Even if we ignore such complications, there is the point
made by Feinberg (1975: 134) that:

> . . . the harm principle is a largely empty formula in urgent need of
> supplementation by tests for determining the relative importance of
> conflicting interests and by measures of the degree to which interests
> are endangered by free expressions.

Probably the single most significant way of supplementing the harm principle is via application of the so-called 'clear and present danger' test.
According to this test it must be shown that the unrestricted expression
of certain views or information would create a clear and present danger
of generating substantive harm. This test obviously makes the context
of an utterance or other form of expression a critical consideration. Nevertheless the test obviously needs to be interpreted in such a way that it
cannot be abused. No government should be permitted to appeal to the
test simply as a means to silencing those who oppose that government.
Totalitarian and repressive governments are too apt to claim that what
their opponents say (e.g. in speeches advocating the overthrow of such
governments) poses a clear and present danger. If this test is to be applied at all it must be applied stringently, but when it is it rules out only
the most extreme forms of incitement. Since the test has to do with *harm*
(as distinct from offensiveness) it would be improper to infringe on the
freedom of expression of citizens in the absence of a properly made out
and well substantiated account of the threatened harms and their impact
on relevant interests.

An appropriate illustration of a situation where such an account might
be given would be one where members of the National Front or of the
Ku Klux Klan wish to march through an area heavily populated with blacks
and to make inflammatory speeches about the inferior status of blacks,
the need to teach them a lesson about whose country it is that they live
in and so forth. In such an instance there is, as recent history testifies,
a very real likelihood of riots and consequent injury and damage to property. The 'clear and present danger' test might mandate intervention by
the relevant authorities even though this would involve restricting the
autonomy of the marchers. Of course, an alternative venue which promised no threat of riots might allow a defensible measure of autonomy
for the marchers.

Although there are situations where the harm test and the clear and
present danger test may be helpful, there are others where the promise
of helpfulness ultimately proves chimerical. Consider a hard case in the

commercial sphere. What are we to say about the liberty of a manufac-
turer (an individual let us say, rather than a corporation) to advertise
cigarettes in theatres, on television, at sports arenas and the like? Recently
this liberty has been under attack in various places and has been removed in others. Is its removal a justifiable use of state power? The clear
and present danger test might seem to imply that it is, given the availability
of medical studies on the harmful effects of cigarette smoking. But this
seeming implication would be rejected by those who stress the sovereignty
of the individual in deciding what to believe, in weighing information
about those beliefs and so forth (cf. Mill, *On Liberty*, ch. 2; Meiklejohn
1965). Any restriction on the freedom of expression of the advertiser
would be opposed because it would be held to rest on an unwarranted
paternalistic interference with the autonomy of those to whom the message
is directed, the audience. Is there any way of resolving this disagreement?

T.M. Scanlon (1979) has outlined a theory which gives some promise
of helping resolve such disagreements. He makes the point that the protection to which an act of expression is entitled is a function in part of
the value of the larger purposes it serves as measured by the *categories
of interests* ('participant', 'audience', 'bystander') that it involves. Recognition of the various categories of acts of expression is largely a matter
of intent and content. Not surprisingly, this often makes for controversy
about the category of an expressive activity. Such indeterminacy contributes to the problems faced by communities in trying to regulate one
category of speech without restricting others as well. Given these difficulties Scanlon believes special notice must be taken of the categories
of interest that are affected by decisions either to protect or regulate various
forms of expression. The greater the value of the particular categories
of interest at stake (as judged by community consensus) the stronger the
argument for protection of any act of expression which furthers these
interests.

Scanlon's complex theory may be applied in difficult cases (like that
of the freedom to advertise cigarettes) where there are profound
disagreements within the community about the justifiability of protecting freedom of expression. Scanlon makes several suggestions (1979: 541)
about why commercial speech may be subject to restrictions that would
not be acceptable if applied to other forms of expression. First, the participant and audience interests at stake in commercial speech (promotion of business and consumer information) are, as things stand, liber-
ally provided for and opportunities for expression are fairly distributed.
Second, since there are reasonably clear and objective criteria of truth
for what constitutes false or misleading advertising, audience interests

can be legally protected. Such a measure of paternalism is acceptable in a way that it would not be in relation to, say, misleading claims in the political or religious spheres. Third, there is less reason to question the motives of a government which imposes restrictions on the advertising of cigarettes than there would be were a government to try to muzzle the expression of political or religious views. This is because these latter categories have to do with more important interests, interests whose importance stems from their centrality to personal autonomy. Considerations of these three kinds would seem to justify the placing of some restrictions on the advertising of cigarettes.

Though Scanlon's approach is a helpful one across a wide range of problem cases for freedom of expression, the prominence he accords to important participant and audience interests would sometimes permit expressions which should not be permitted. It would seem, for instance, that on his theory the National Front march mentioned earlier would be permissible (see e.g. 1979: 519f, 539 and compare Skillen 1982: 143ff). While there are important participant interests here (and perhaps even audience ones) because this is a matter of political expression, there are also very important bystander interests. Some place must, therefore, be found for a balancing of interests — the sort of thing which Scanlon (1979: 534) wishes to avoid. Such a balancing of interests would require that the march at least be routed through an area less likely to be a flashpoint.

But this is not to gainsay the fact that Scanlon's general approach is a constructive one, even if it is not the whole story. This can be further illustrated by considering one final 'hard case', that to do with when to permit the expression of pornographic ideas. It is sometimes argued that to permit the expression of such ideas would be harmful. There is, however, very little empirical evidence to support such a claim for, although few researchers doubt that the expression of such ideas may influence certain persons who subsequently harm others, establishing the appropriate kind of causal link is immensely problematic (cf. Schauer 1982: ch. 12, Feinberg 1984: ch. 6). Recently, some feminists have urged that because pornographic material treats women as sex objects, and being thought of as a sex object is to be a harmed object, pornography harms women (cf. Brownmiller 1975; Garry 1978). Others including some feminists, reject this claim as being too sweeping or as depending on contentious psychological claims about what people (especially men) experience while looking at pornographic material.

Many have thought it more promising to look instead to the principle of offensiveness as grounds for restricting pornography (certainly for 'unwilling audiences' if not more generally). According to this principle it is a relevant consideration in deciding the permissibility of a person's conduct whether his (or her) manner of expression (including speech) has the capacity to cause unpleasant or distressing mental states such as disgust, shocked sensibilities, repugnance and shameful embarrassment in those who witness it (or hear it, smell it . . .), even though it will not generate physical harm (cf. Feinberg 1973a and 1979a; Bayles 1973; Van De Veer 1979). Before considering the circumstances in which this principle would justify limiting an offender's autonomy, it must first be seen that the principle only covers some of the issues relevant to the question of restricting the merchant of pornography.

First, methods to keep *unwilling* audiences away from confrontations with offensive pornography would, in practice, involve very little restriction on the circulation or display of such material, let alone prohibition (Williams 1979). Moreover, as Scanlon has argued (1979: 545f) if people are entitled to a fair opportunity to influence the (sexual) *mores* of their society, as undoubtedly some partisans of pornography wish, then 'it seems that they, like participants in political speech in the narrow sense, are entitled to at least a certain degree of access even to unwilling audiences' (cp. R. Dworkin 1968; Berger 1977). It would, I take it, be fair to presume that reasonable avoidability would remain possible as it does in the parallel political case. Even the 'reasonable avoidability standard' may, however, be set at nought in cases such as the mounting of vicious, ridiculing attacks in the mass media on minority groups. This is because such attacks would violate other relevant standards like those of 'reasonable restraint' and require more than 'normal permissiveness towards conscientiously motivated offence'. (Cf. Van De Veer 1979: 185ff.)

But even if those who seek to change others' attitudes have participant interests of the sort mentioned there are audience interests to be taken into account as well. The difficulty in doing so, as Scanlon points out (1979: 548f), relates to whether protection can be given to audience interests 'without unacceptably restricting other persuasive activity'. How, for instance, to draw the line between the campaigner on behalf of pornography and the campaigner against participation in war who insists that without the freedom to show unexpurgated scenes of violence he (or she) will be unable to persuade fellow citizens of the wrongness of participation in a particular war? One might have expected Scanlon to appeal to the greater importance of the category into which the second case falls. But instead he takes the view that it is not possible to restrict the one without restricting the other. However, even if he is right on this score, little if any pornography is so high-minded (cf. Skillen 1982a) and the floodgates would not be opened.

Accordingly, it seems necessary to engage in the difficult business of balancing interests. We shall, therefore, consider several of the more likely guidelines as to when the fact of something's offending others (by causing unpleasant or distressing mental states) *would* justify restricting the offender's autonomy. 'Guidelines' appears apt, since it is doubtful that a clear 'rule' covering the appropriate instances can be formulated.

The first consideration is that people must actually be offended. Moreover, the person offended must not be so placed as to be able easily and effectively to avoid being offended. This is important because in circumstances where the likely offensive behaviour, display or whatever *is* readily avoidable (e.g. in a book or film; on a programme on only one radio station or television channel; occurs in a private place such as one's home or in an out of the way place like a secluded beach), its mere potential to offend is no ground for regulation. Moreover, the inclusion of this guideline has the advantage of building in a degree of social and cultural flexibility. What is found offensive varies over time and from place to place.

A second point, closely related to the first, is that any offence felt must be felt not for idiosyncratic reasons peculiar to one or a few individuals, but by a significant segment of the population. 'Significant' rather than, for instance, 'overwhelming' segment, copes with two sources of difficulty for the stronger claim: first the extent to which convictions vary in multi-cultural societies about the typical causes for concern, and, second, the complexities introduced when convictions about certain matters are in turmoil because of rapid changes in social *mores*. Even so, there is disagreement about this issue. Feinberg defends the view that except where the potentially offensive behaviour consists in abusive, mocking or insulting behaviour, intervention is permissible only when serious offence may reasonably be expected in *anyone* chosen at random from the general populace. But a serious weakness in this view is that the exceptions clause is too easily met and hence is at odds with the requirements of the 'offends almost any one chosen at random' clause.

There are those who think that this should lead to our giving due consideration to those who are offended, even when their sensibilities are bizarre or unreasonable, because vulnerability to distress does have some moral weight. Van De Veer (1979: 184f) endeavours to support such a proposal by arguing that the case is analogous to the idea of a bizarre sensibility in the vulnerability of some people to rare allergies and afflictions. These two cases, however, are not quite as close as Van De Veer suggests. The person with the unusual sensitivity to some substance will suffer *physical harm* if others fail to take steps to avoid upsetting him or her. The weight to be accorded to such suffering is, presumably, greater than that for distress occasioned by offence. Van De Veer is right to hold that distress occasioned by offence has some moral weight. But since the law is an instrument of social policy, it would not be an appropriate means for recognition of this moral weight. The two-part conclusion to be drawn is (a) that individuals act in a morally proper fashion where they show extra consideration and restraint in view of the fact that their activities may place third parties with unusual sensibilities at risk, but equally (b) that legal sanctions are out of place in such cases.

Third, any offence felt must not be of a trivial sort. One or more of the range of emotions mentioned earlier on — disgust, shocked sensibilities, repugnance, shameful embarrassment — must be experienced. It is not enough for one to take offence, say, at public nudity, where the reason for one's disgust is that the bodies on display are unaesthetic and that better ones should have been pressed into service.

Fourth, the existence of any personal or social worth in the activity, work of art, or whatever, has to be given proper consideration. The presence of personal or social worth in an activity which some none the less find offensive should be sufficient to tip the scales in favour of permitting the activity. There is a world of difference between a performance in a public park by a modern ballet troupe dancing nude and a no-holds barred demonstration, in the same setting, of the services available at a nearby brothel. The intention of the offender thus bears on whether the action should be permitted (cp. Feinberg 1973a and Bayles 1973). This is a battle that has been fought many a time in relation to the autonomy of the literary artist. None the less, there is one feature of the literary case which is thought by some to show the two cases to be quite different. In the literary case clearly there is reasonable avoidability for those not wishing to be confronted with potentially offensive material. In the nude ballet case, this is not so. An adjustment to the case which covers the worry is easily made. If the ballet troupe had previously advertised its performance or were perhaps to erect notices in the park near to the time of the performance, the cases would be more in line with each other.

It may be thought that this adjustment brings with it the unintended consequence of making permissible the demonstration of sexual services available at the local brothel. This is not so — or at least not obviously so — because the other guidelines advanced would need to be taken into account. Once they were it would be possible to show that the fairest way to balance the competing interests would be to restrict the autonomy of the demonstrators (or to pre-empt the exercise of their autonomy in this particular regard).

A closely related but distinct issue which sometimes arises in discussions about freedom of expression concerns 'nuisances'. Sometimes people are 'put out' rather than offended by an activity. Suppose, for example, the playing of loud rock music in a park mainly frequented by elderly citizens is so noisy as to upset the elderly citizens and to drive them away. This would fall under the heading of 'nuisance'. With nuisances what is normally required is an accommodation (rather than a balancing) of all relevant interests and so the issues raised are less troublesome. In the example given, a scheme would need to be worked out to give reasonable access to the facilities to all interested parties. Only where such an accommodation cannot be reached is there liable to be thought of legal action to restrain the offender, or in the extreme to obtain damages (cp. Hart and Honoré 1959: 211ff).

IV

The discussion of the limits on other-regarding autonomous behaviour has taken account of harm and offence as effects produced by positive action. The discussion is incomplete because it is arguable that we may effectively harm others by *failing to act*. Suppose, for instance, *R* fails to render aid to *S* when *R* could easily and without much cost have done so, and *S* suffers injury in consequence. Some writers would say that *R* has harmed *S*, others that *R*'s omission renders *R* responsible for any ensuing harm to *S* (cf. Harris 1974, 1980 and 1982; Kleinig 1976; Singer 1980, ch. 8; Feinberg 1984, ch. 4; *pace* Mack 1980; Weinryb 1980). It is not necessary to engage in a full-scale discussion of this issue since our present concern is only with imposing legitimate *limitations* on autonomy for other-regarding reasons; clearly, many instances of failure to prevent injury will not come realistically within that brief. But some no doubt will. For instance, it is surely the case that an agent of the government (say a policeman or rescue worker) should be able to require reasonable assistance from a citizen in an emergency or to commandeer his (or her) property. The citizen may not omit to offer reasonable assistance in such circumstances even though this will infringe on his (or her) autonomy. Nor are we permitted to refuse to fulfil certain other kinds of obligation. Thus governments impose taxes on citizens to enable them to spend on general welfare measures and thereby to reduce or prevent injury and suffering. Only the libertarian voice (such as Nozick 1974: ch. 7) is raised against such government activities (though there are many dissenting voices as regards levels of taxation and various ways in which governments spend tax revenues for purposes like defence that are only dubiously to be thought of as providing a welfare benefit).

The rationale for such government action is not hard to see: without it the fundamental interests (like welfare interests) of some individuals will not be met and they will be harmed, whereas the 'surplus' funds creamed off from those on higher incomes, or with greater wealth, will not render them unable to satisfy their fundamental interests. Such a rationale is clearly consistent with the pervasive theme of the limitations on autonomy argued in this chapter to be legitimate, namely that of producing the fairest balance of interests among all those affected. Any failure, in practice, to achieve this goal, is a ground for criticising the means rather than the end.

8 LIMITING AUTONOMY: ECONOMIC RELATIONS

Market exchanges, and economic exchanges in general, constitute an important class of actions. They bear importantly on all of our lives. The question of whether they are to be subject to the strictures of the private harm principle elaborated in the previous chapter therefore assumes no little importance. It may seem straightforward enough that since such actions are other-regarding, and so may harmfully affect the interests of others, the strictures of the private harm principle do apply. In at least one place in *On Liberty* (1963 vol. 18: 293) Mill appears to endorse this suggestion *in principle*. He goes on, however, to claim that in practice it is better not to regulate trade. The sole check needed to ensure equal freedom for producers, sellers and buyers is the operation of 'free trade'. This doctrine of free trade rests, he claims, on 'grounds different from, though equally solid with, the principle of individual liberty'. The effect of Mill's position in *On Liberty* is that there will be little ground for regulation of economic activity. (By the time, however, that Mill came to write 'Chapters on Socialism' (1963 vol 5: 727ff) he was not quite as sanguine about the extent to which free trade was operative.)

If we suppose the institution of private property and the operation of a competitive market, where goods exchanged have not wrongfully been come by and where the exchange is fully voluntary (there being no force, fraud, deception or the like), any restrictions imposed on such market exchanges will represent an unwarranted intrusion on the economic liberty of the trading partners. (Cf. Hayek 1960, 1973, 1976, 1979; Friedman, M. 1962; Friedman, M. and Friedman, R. 1980; Rothbard 1973; Nozick 1974.) Regulation has its place when the goods exchanged were wrongfully come by or when the exchange is not fully voluntary, since these things involve using others against their will for one's own purposes, which is a grave wrong. Otherwise a person's autonomy is to be thought of as an enabling condition for the use of his (or her) property in those enterprises he favours.

Since the market mechanism is supposed to ensure that any costs to other affected parties are taken into account, regulation really has no place save to protect the interests of parties directly involved in the trading. If no one else *is* affected, to prevent exchanges where none of the grounds for interference previously mentioned is present, is Pareto inefficient. This is because the trading partners are stopped from moving to more preferred positions and, thereby, from making the final outcome nearer to Pareto optimality than that at which the exchange took place (cf. Scanlon 1977: 43f).

On such an account, the primacy of personal autonomy, especially as regards economic choice and action, demands an economy relatively free of legal and governmental direction as long as force, fraud and deception are not prevalent. In particular it demands an economic structure which operates with little government interference (i.e. is a private enterprise system) and is competitive. This is a position firmly within the individualist tradition. The position's supporters hold that government power and activity must be reduced if individual autonomy is to be promoted. They believe as well that not only will greater economic liberty enhance overall autonomy for those individuals, it will also produce significant material enrichment all round.

To discuss this last claim with any seriousness would take us too far afield. It is worth noting, though, that critics of economic individualism strongly dispute the claim (cf. for example, Cohen 1978: ch. 11). Discussion, however, of virtually all of the other claims cited cannot be avoided, if we are to decide whether restrictions on the economic liberty or autonomy of some individuals are needed to prevent harm to others. Of particular interest is whether the restrictions need to include protections against such loss of control by individuals over their own lives as may follow from the exercise of others' economic liberties.

In what follows it is argued that private ownership of the means of production in a market economy *is* a powerful constraint on the individual's capacity to shape his (or her) life. Unless restrictions are imposed on the economic liberty of individuals (and consortiums) the autonomy of others will be jeopardised. If the argument is sound it will provide legitimate other-regarding grounds for restricting the economic liberty of individuals. This contrasts with Nozick's insistence (1974: 334) that millionaires may not legitimately be taxed to provide subsidised milk for the poor, since such taxation would violate their rights.

The argument as presented must, however, be acknowledged to be incomplete because there is not space here to consider how far-reaching the regulation of individual economic activity must be to achieve a fair balance of autonomy for all. Some authors (e.g. Rawls 1971; Gutmann 1980) contend that a like autonomy for all would be achievable in a carefully regulated private enterprise society. Others hold that significant protection of the autonomy of all would require the development of community ownership of the means of production (cf. Cohen 1977: 14; 1981: 235ff; Gould 1978: ch. 1). To do justice to these competing claims would among other things require the sifting of available empirical evidence about the effects on individual autonomy of private ownership of the means of production as against public or community ownership. Quite apart from the fact that the available evidence on these matters is patchy, a work of the present sort is not the place to do the sifting referred to above. Despite its incompleteness, the argument does establish that nothing less than a highly regulated version of a private enterprise economy will be effective in preserving the autonomy of the many. That is undoubtedly a conclusion of significance for those who value personal autonomy.

I

Hitherto, we have referred to 'economic liberty' rather than to 'economic autonomy', where the latter expression might have appeared more apposite. The use of 'economic liberty', however, better conveys the fact that economic goals and concerns, while significant, do not form the heart and soul, and certainly do not exhaust, the content of the life-plans of most people.

As for the meaning to be attached to economic liberty, there are different views. One of the more common of these has certain parallels with the notion of 'negative liberty'. It is to the effect that economic liberty consists in not being restricted either in selling what one owns or in buying what one wants (Narveson, 1976). This view suffers from the narrowness common to 'negative' characterisations of liberty. Moreover, it does not accord very well with the understanding of economic liberty to which libertarians, at least, are committed. The libertarian commitment to the institution of private property comprehends, not just a liberty to buy and sell, but equally (and more broadly) the liberty to *use* one's goods and services. Robert Nozick (1974: 167), for instance, makes much of the difficulty he alleges socialists have with permitting gift-giving. He takes it that any commitment to equality of distribution, to be achieved by placing upper limits on the accumulation of wealth, violates the right to bestow gifts. In the Wilt Chamberlain example discussed below, Nozick hypothesises that the many may freely choose to transfer some portion of their resources to a very few, thereby producing an inegalitarian distribution. The point is not about the inevitability, even desirability, of unequal distribution. (See the rather different considerations pressed by Swanton 1979 and Rawls 1971: 203, 244.) The point rather is that Nozick, a libertarian, conceives economic liberty as according a comprehensive right of use, and not just an absence of restrictions on buying and selling. In this, he provides a common point of departure that might usefully be adopted by socialists, liberals and libertarians, and is accordingly used here.

The problem to which we must now attend concerns the conditions whose satisfaction would produce greater economic liberty for individuals, and, in consequence, more control by individuals over their own lives. Given the extent of usurpation of property, of fraud, of deception, of theft and so on in previous generations, and given the way in which inheritance laws work to protect such gains, the requirement that the goods which people now have available to use *not have been wrongfully come by*, seems impossible of satisfaction. Notoriously, of course, discussions of such facts are not the economic individualist's strength. Nozick's discussion, for instance, of principles of rectification (1974: 230f) is hardly satisfying. Moreover, along with many others of his persuasion, he does not see such facts as casting serious doubt on central libertarian claims.

What we must determine is whether there can be any autonomy or liberty-based grounds for restricting economic exchanges consistent with the retention of private property, a competitive market, and the exchanges being fully voluntary. We may begin by considering some of the effects of the institution of private property on economic liberty and, by implication, autonomy. Let us say, if some good belongs to R, that S ceases to be free to use it for economic (or any other) purposes unless given permission by R. This point is obvious and will not readily be disputed. Property rules do exclude non-owners (where permission is withheld) from the use of property. (Although of no immediate relevance, it is also true that laws often restrict what owners themselves may do with their property.) Restrictions on the use of goods (save by permission) are not, however, the effect of *private* property specifically, but of property in general. The issue we must address is whether a system of private property significantly reduces the liberty of non-owners (Cohen 1979: 13f; 1981: 226ff; Steiner 1980: 260).

In the private enterprise economies with which we are familiar, the existence of property rights, particularly over the 'factors of production' (such as land, raw materials, natural resources, capital equipment and labour), gives rise to a situation in which a large proportion of people, in order to obtain their livelihood, require both to use these factors of production and to place themselves under the control of those who own them (cf. Scanlon 1977: 62; Cohen 1981: 224). (It is as well to note that 'labour', for our purposes, is too encompassing a category, since it must also include those, for example, whose rare talents accord them relative advantage in market conditions *vis-à-vis* those with only their everyday labour power to sell.)

In a private enterprise market economy, the outlook for a good many people — for those, namely, who have only their labour power to sell (along, of course, with the dependents of such people), or who are unable to find a buyer for their labour, or who are unable any longer to work — is to be, or remain, subject to the control of those who own and control the land, natural resources and so forth in such an economy. In these circumstances, the Lockean provisos — conditions to the effect that those appropriating land or natural resources should leave enough and as good for others and acquire no more than can be utilised without waste (Locke 1963: ch. 5, paras. 27, 31, pp. 328f, 332) — are not satisfied.

The loss of autonomy suffered by the average individual in a free enterprise economy is probably greater than it would be in altered circumstances where *either* the 'economic rent' an individual could command for his scarce talents was regulated, *or* where limits were imposed on the extent of his (and everyone else's) holdings (Scanlon 1976: 13ff; 1977: 63f; Loevinsohn 1977: 229-37). The net effect of these altered arrangements would, of course, be to restrict the autonomy of some, in the sense that certain individuals would be less free than before to control such concentrations of scarce resources as would enable them to hold undue power over the life prospects of others. But the loss of autonomy by some may serve as a ground for gains by others, just as the abolition of slavery reduces the autonomy of slave-owners, but, in doing so, enhances that of former slaves. In each case some individuals suffer a loss in autonomy, others gain in fundamental aspects of autonomy. The net effect is a fairer balance.

There are several counter-arguments available to those who are concerned to oppose greater control over the operations of a private enterprise system. One of the most recent of these is the Wilt Chamberlain example devised by Nozick, the burden of which is that voluntary exchanges basically expand, rather than restrict, our freedom, and, indeed, that markedly unequal distributions of goods and services may directly and legitimately flow from such free exchanges.

In Nozick's example, Wilt Chamberlain's great crowd-drawing capacity among basketball enthusiasts enables him to negotiate a highly favourable contract. The terms are that Chamberlain keeps 25 cents from the price of each admission for the games in which he plays. This 25 cents is clearly earmarked for Chamberlain, so fans know full well where their money is going. A million tickets are sold during the season and Chamberlain becomes a quarter of a million dollars better off. (Given what sports stars can command in the US today, Nozick's figures are rather outdated, but a quarter of a million dollars remains a significant resource.) Nozick writes:

> Each of these persons *chose* to give twenty-five cents of their money to Chamberlain. They could have spent it on going to the movies, or on candy bars, or on copies of *Dissent* magazine, or of *Monthly Review*. But they all, at least one million of them, converged on giving it to Wilt Chamberlain in exchange for watching him play basketball (1974: 161f, Nozick's emphasis).

Nozick assumes the Chamberlain fans to be rational in acting as they do because they perceive what they do to be beneficial to themselves (cp. Cohen, 1977: 8). Nozick does not say enough to indicate whether he accepts the assumption commonly made in theoretical economics that 'economic man' is guided *only* by self-interest. Since he favours charity (one presumes unself-interested charity) it is possible that he does not. (For a critique of the assumption see Sen 1977.)

It may be that the fans benefit in the way they anticipate. But that is not all that happens. As Cohen observes (1977: 9) the fans may not appreciate the full consequences of their actions. One of the possible outcomes of the payment to Chamberlain is that he may come to occupy a position of power and influence over and above that of the ordinary person (bearing in mind that the example is set in a society with an egalitarian distribution of existing wealth). The upshot, once the point is generalised, is the establishment of classes that are unequally wealthy and powerful, such that some are systematically required to work for and to depend upon others. In this way, Wilt's fans get more than they bargained for.

This is how Cohen (1977: 11) puts it:

> Nozick tacitly supposes that a person willing to pay twenty-five cents to watch Wilt play is *ipso facto* a person willing to pay *Wilt* twenty-five cents to watch him play. It is no doubt true that in our society people rarely care who gets the money they forgo to obtain goods. But the tacit supposition is false, and the common unconcern is irrational. Nozick exploits our familiarity with this unconcern. Yet a person might welcome a world in which he and a million others watch Wilt play, at a cost of twenty-five cents to each, and consistently disfavour one in which, in addition, Wilt receives a cool quarter million (Cohen's emphasis).

The point is that voluntary exchanges do not always expand our freedom and that, where they create considerable inequality, it is not to be assumed that this outcome is either necessary or desired by the participants.

Aside from the complaint which I have indicated earlier cannot be dealt with properly in this book, namely the charge made by Hayek, Friedman, Rothbard and Nozick that we would all, or nearly all, have far less autonomy under socialist economic arrangements, there is a separate response made by such thinkers to arguments like the preceding one. It is made explicitly by Hayek (1960: ch. 1) and by Nozick (1974: 262–4). Let us consider Nozick's account. Nozick holds that a person is forced to choose between working (for a capitalist, say) in order to obtain the means to life, and starving, only if (roughly) his alternatives are restricted by some other person's acting in a way that violates his rights.

It is, of course, just false that only the actions, let alone only the illegitimate actions, of other persons render an individual's choices unfree. Circumstances, too, can impose on an individual's will (cf. Frankfurt 1973: 83f; Crocker 1980: ch. 4). The construction Nozick and others like Hayek have placed on what it is to have one's choices made unfree is too narrow. In Chapter 4 it was pointed out that 'external negative constraints' (like lacks in resources) can restrict people's autonomy by, for instance, restricting their opportunities.

Nozick's commitment to private property in the means of production and the rights of owners to which this institution gives rise, has the effect of setting up an important asymmetry between 'workers' and 'employers'. He contends that interference with the rights of owners who do not resort to unfairness or wrongdoing in their dealings with workers, would be like forcible reassignment of marriage partners (1974: 262–5). Such a contention entrenches an asymmetry in the power relations between employers and workers, the former being given an unacceptable degree of control over the latter. Economic liberty for those who own the means of production within a private enterprise economy, especially a thoroughly libertarian one, imposes constraints on the liberty of those who do not.

Of course it may be said that under a true free enterprise system it is possible for all (or at least many more than do) to 'rise' to a position where they themselves own or have a significant share in the means of production. But there is no empirical evidence to substantiate the claim that any more than a small proportion do alter their 'class position'. Some succeed because of sheer industry, notably a willingness to work long hours in trading on their own behalf. Some, like sportspersons or entertainers, may have a scarce, readily marketable talent which can command a premium. Success may come to innovators who are early entrants into new fields as has happened in electronics. Some may manage by means of windfall gains from speculative investments made from an initially small bank-roll and so forth. But the numbers who 'make it' remain relatively small, and this is necessarily so from the standpoint of the non-owning class as a whole (cf. Sennett and Cobb 1972; Cohen 1982). It may be true that these openings are open to all, but this is only in the weak sense that no individual is *prohibited* from seeking them. Non-owner individuals, for all that, remain members of a *class* whose freedom of opportunity is severely constrained. (Gerald Cohen (1982: 9f; cf. Zimmerman 1981: 138f) nicely illustrates this point.)

II

Part of the case presented on behalf of competitive capitalism by economic individualists is that the unfettered operation of market forces makes for an expansion in individual choice. The argument presented above can be strengthened by showing that this claim of economic individualists is as unsustainable as their more general contention that unrestricted economic liberty enhances overall autonomy.

Once we look on people not merely as consumers, but also as workers and as citizens, it is not hard to see that whatever additional choice a consumer may have as a result of living in a competitive market situation diminishes in significance if at the same time choice of physical and social environment is reduced. Such reduction of choice, stemming mainly from so-called 'external diseconomies' or 'spillover costs', eats into and may wipe out any advantage from expansion in consumer choices. Some spillover costs like pollution, noise, congestion, toxic wastes and the like have to be borne by all of us as citizens; some, such as work-induced diseases, by the few who work in the relevant industries; and some, like future resource scarcities, by generations to come.

Economic individualists are, of course, aware of spillover costs. They contend for the most part that the market is the most efficient means for coping with the incidence of spillovers. They hold, for instance, that scarce resources (like land, bodies of water and so forth) are best protected by placing them under exclusive private ownership and allowing their owners to charge an economic rent for their use. The imposition by a central authority of strategies to reduce the impact of spillovers, which the socialist, for instance, puts up as a contrasting approach, or the establishment of interventionist bodies such as environmental protection agencies in 'mixed' economies is alleged to reduce freedom and involve a net economic loss (because, it would make necessary the relocation of some industries, stop some forms of production, and make for expensive 'reorganisation costs'). As already indicated, it is not possible to consider all of the issues which this reply raises. However, several points can be made about the way in which spillover costs diminish the autonomy of those who suffer such costs.

First, extending property rights is unlikely to protect scarce resources against over-exploitation. Indeed there is plenty of evidence to suggest the contrary — witness what has happened with non-renewable resources such as fossil fuels and certain mineral ores. Future generations will have to bear the costs of this accelerated depletion.

Second, there are many instances where the vital interests of individual citizens are adversely affected as a result of the cumulative impact on the environment of the activities of numerous parties ('acid rain' is a case in point). In isolation the contributions of the individual parties may be 'harmless'. It is the cumulative effect of all the contributions which harms the affected citizens. To ban those property holders contributing to the problem from carrying on their activities may be undesirable since it is conceivable that each would be justifiable in isolation. To expect the affected citizens to take steps to protect their interests may be unrealistic since the cost of doing so is likely to be prohibitive. Despite such difficulties, those citizens who are exposed to harm (and thus to a loss of their autonomy) must have some recourse to protect their interests if each citizen's autonomy is to be accorded equal worth. Some writers (e.g. Macpherson 1977: 72ff) argue that if citizens are to be thought of as having individual rights in the environment they can take exploiters to court for despoliation. Even if the prohibitive cost of doing so could be overcome by way of class actions, some violations of the rights of citizens will be such that compensation is not feasible (e.g. lasting effects on health). In circumstances of this latter kind prevention may be the only cure.

Third, the presumption that what a competitive market licenses is necessarily beneficial, runs counter to the fact that many products have harmful effects which are invisible until it is too late to do anything about them. Much else that is produced is manifestly of no real value but may yet be produced because people can be induced to buy. The market has to be seen as limited in its capacity to deliver the right judgements about the kinds of goods and services that ought to be produced. It is subject to distortion by those with concentrated holdings of wealth and does not take account of moral factors.

III

The pursuit of economic individualist ideals in a competitive market economy with private property, diminishes personal autonomy for most citizens. This is too great a price to pay for the increased autonomy available to those with sufficient resources to avoid being subject to any significant degree to the will of others. The point is not that there is too much freedom under competitive capitalism. It is that there is too much for some people, too little for others and hence that a like autonomy is not available to all. Many, though by no means all, citizens of private enterprise societies enjoy various freedoms (such as freedom of religious affiliation, of political participation and so forth). This fact suggests that more than just capitalist economic arrangements but as well historical and cultural traditions, for instance, bear on whether these freedoms will be available. These various freedoms are things any society worth belonging to (and hence including those which replace private ownership of the means of production with communal ownership) should also cherish.

The replacement of private ownership in the means of production clearly involves some reduction in the degree of autonomy previously enjoyed by the private owners — but the point of thus restricting some people's autonomy is to make for a society in which all can exercise a like degree of control over their lives. Capitalism protects certain liberties, chiefly those connected with the ownership of private property. The socialist claims there is a need to protect the autonomy of individuals in a much wider way. Interventionist liberals frequently are also motivated by the desire to increase general autonomy. That is why they, like socialists, are critical of the libertarian concern to protect particular economic liberties, especially those to do with private property, even where this exacts its cost as losses in autonomy for others. Socialists contend that the interventionist liberal does not go far enough in the regulation of capitalism and thus that concentrations of economic power will remain which militate against the autonomy of the members of the worst-off sections of society. So, when liberals like Mill, Green, Hobhouse and Rawls argue that a good society is one in which a state of affairs is actively promoted that would equip each person to pursue his (or her) own good because, by and large, autonomy generates welfare, the dispute with socialists is not over this goal but its attainability in private enterprise economies which are merely subject to government regulation (rather than transformed) as against its attainability in actual socialist economies.

9 CONCLUSION

The traditional model of the autonomous political state, as a state free from external governance, is an unsatisfactory basis for thinking about personal autonomy. Foremost among the reasons for its unsatisfactoriness is that autonomy does not merely consist in being unobstructed in one's pursuits. To be thus unobstructed is necessary, but not sufficient. To exercise autonomy, certain positive qualities are also required, viz. the possession of rational capacities, strength of will and, for certain purposes, self-knowledge. To be autonomous is to author one's world, and this goes beyond simply being free from obstructions.

Lives are the primary referents in talk of autonomy. To author one's world is to shape and direct one's life. There is a legitimate sense in which a person can occurrently act autonomously. But judgements about personal autonomy are centrally dispositional: they relate to a person's following through on a plan or conception of his (or her) life which unifies his various pursuits.

Personal autonomy thus conceived is valuable for its own sake as well as for the achievements it can make possible. It is intrinsically valuable because it provides the foundation of moral personhood and gives us dignity and standing as moral agents. We can, of course, exercise our autonomy for both good and ill. When an individual's autonomy is ill-used, we may judge that, the intrinsic value of autonomy notwithstanding, it would have been better (all things considered) had his (or her) autonomy not been exercised in that way. It may be necessary to respond by restricting such exercises of autonomy. Indeed, where the exercise of autonomy poses a serious risk of ill effect, it may be better to check its exercise. There is wide agreement on these points on the grounds that each person's autonomy is of like value to every other, whence the conclusion that no individual should be permitted to exercise his (or her) autonomy in ways that jeopardise the autonomy of others. The implications of this widely agreed principle are more far-reaching than is generally recognised.

The equal worth of each person's autonomy has always been the centrepiece of individualism (whether of the liberal or the libertarian form). Individuals have the right, according to this tradition, to make of their lives whatever they choose. As Mill put it in *On Liberty* (226): '. . . mankind are greater gainers by suffering each other to live as seems good to themselves, than by compelling each other to live as seems good to the rest.' It would seem to be an implication of this position that the individual also has a right to lead his (or her) own life free of the demand constantly to promote the best overall results (cf. Nagel 1979: 84; Scheffler 1982: 34f).

The individualist tradition has not always been faithful to the idea that each individual's autonomy is of equal value with every other's. Serious losses in autonomy for some are often engendered by permitting the economic individualism of others. No one of us can, in fairness, be wholly autonomous and hence we must seek a fair overall balance of autonomy. What people do in their economic life has flow-on effects to other spheres of life if only because the wealth and income obtained through economic activities affect opportunities to pursue other interests (cf. Bowles and Gintis 1976).

It is not, however, just the actions of other individuals in producing or threatening harm, nor the tendency of an economic system based on private property to generate systematic losses in the autonomy of the property-less through exploitation, which may necessitate imposing restrictions on the ways in which individuals may pursue their life-plans. An agent's own actions may threaten to undermine his (or her) subsequent exercise of autonomy in matters that are fundamental to his life-plan. While paternalistic interferences with autonomy have been judged by many liberals and libertarians to be despotic and insulting (Berlin 1969: 157), they are sometimes necessary to protect and preserve the very scope for exercising dispositional autonomy to which such critics are pledged. To manage this is neither despotic nor insulting but autonomy enhancing.

The points recapped in the previous few paragraphs are controversial because they indicate commonly unacknowledged ways in which the exercise of autonomy at one time and place may, despite its value and claim to protection, be inimical to a like exercise by others, or even by the agent acting at a later time and another place. To the extent that they are right they bear out the single most important contention in this work: that individualism is deficient.

Individualism is doubly deficient. It neglects the *social* situation of the individual, *and* it neglects the concerns of individuals *in the round*.

Does stressing these deficiencies devalue the individual? Decidedly not. This book has been an attempt to elaborate a conception of personal autonomy which is distinct from that favoured by the individualist tradition. At the same time it has maintained a high view of the value of personal autonomy and of its importance as a character ideal.

BIBLIOGRAPHY

Adams, R.M. (1979) 'Autonomy and Theological Ethics', *Religious Studies*, *15*, 191–4
Archer, R. (1976) 'Personal Autonomy and Historical Materialism', *Radical Philosophy*, no. 15, 8–14
Aristotle *Politics*
—— *Nicomachean Ethics*
Arneson, R. (1980) 'Mill versus Paternalism', *Ethics*, *90*, 470–89
—— (1981) 'Prospects for Community in a Market Economy', *Political Theory*, *9*, 207–27
Arrow, K. (1963) *Social Choice and Individual Values*, London
Audi, R. (1979) 'Weakness of Will and Practical Judgement', *Nous*, *13*, 173–96
Aune, B. (1979) *Kant's Theory of Morals*, Princeton, N.J.
Bailey, J. (1979) 'On Intrinsic Value', *Philosophia*, *9*, 1–8
Barrow, R. (1975) *Moral Philosophy for Education*, London
Barry, B. (1965) *Political Argument*, London
Bayles, M. (1973) 'Comments on Feinberg: Offensive Conduct and the Law' in N.S. Care and K.T. Trelogan (eds.), *Issues in Law and Morality*, Cleveland and London
—— (1974) 'Criminal Paternalism' in *Nomos XV: The Limits of Law*, J.R. Pennock and J.W. Chapman (eds.), New York
—— (1978) *Principles of Legislation*, Detroit
Beardsley, M.C. (1965) 'Intrinsic Value', *Philosophy and Phenomenological Research*, *26*, 1–17
Beauchamp, T. (1977) 'Paternalism and Biobehavioural Control', *The Monist*, *60*, 62–80
—— (1978) 'Paternalism' in *The Encyclopedia of Bioethics*, W.T. Reich (ed.), New York
—— and Childress, J.F. (1979) *Principles of Biomedical Ethics*, New York and Oxford
Benn, S. (1975) 'Freedom, Autonomy and the Concept of a *Person*', *Proceedings of the Aristotelian Society*, *76*, 109–30
—— (1982) 'Individuality, Community and Autonomy', in E. Kamenka (ed.), *Community*, London
—— and Weinstein. W. (1971) 'Being Free to Act and Being a Free Man', *Mind*, *80*, 194–211
Benson, J. (1975) *The Search for the Self*, Lancaster, UK
—— (1983) 'Who Is The Autonomous Man?', *Philosophy*, *58*, 5–17
Berger, F. (1977) 'Pornography, Sex and Censorship', in R. Wasserstrom (ed.), *Today's Moral Problems*, New York and London
Berlin, I. (1969) 'Two Concepts of Liberty', in his *Four Essays on Liberty*, Oxford
Bernstein, M. (1983) 'Socialization and Autonomy', *Mind*, *92*, 120–3
Bettelheim, B. (1960) *The Informed Heart: Autonomy in a Mass Age*, New York
Blackstone, W.T. (1973) 'The Concept of Political Freedom', *Social Theory and Practice*, *2*, 421–38
Block, N. and Dworkin, G. (eds.) (1976) *The I.Q. Controversy*, New York
Blum, L. (1980) *Friendship, Altruism and Morality*, London
Bogen, J. and Farrell, D. (1978) 'Freedom and Happiness in Mill's Defence of Liberty', *Philosophical Quarterly*, *28*, 325–38
Bowles, S. and Gintis, H. (1976) *Schooling in Capitalist America*, New York
Brandt, R. (1959) *Ethical Theory: The Problems of Normative and Critical Ethics*, Englewood Cliffs, N.J.
Brock, D. (1980) 'Involuntary Civil Commitment: The Moral Issues', in B.A. Brody and H.T. Engelhardt (eds.), *Mental Illness: Law and Public Policy*, Dordrecht, Holland
Brownmiller, S. (1975) *Against Our Will: Men, Women and Rape*, New York
Buchheit, L. (1978) *Secession: The Legitimacy of Self-Determination*, New Haven
Campbell, T. (1983) *The Left and Rights: A Conceptual Analysis of the Idea of Socialist*

Rights, London
Carter, R. (1977) 'Justifying Paternalism', *Canadian Journal of Philosophy*, 7, 133–45
Cohen, G.A. (1977) 'Robert Nozick and Wilt Chamberlain: How Patterns Preserve Liberty', *Erkenntnis*, *11*, 5–23
—— (1978) *Karl Marx's Theory of History*, Oxford
—— (1979) 'Capitalism, Freedom and the Proletariat', in A. Ryan (ed.), *The Idea of Freedom: Essays in Honour of Isaiah Berlin*, Oxford
—— (1981) 'Illusions about Private Property and Freedom', in J. Mepham and D. Ruben (eds.), *Issues in Marxist Philosophy*, Hassocks, UK, vol. 4
—— (1982) 'The Structure of Proletarian Unfreedom', *Philosophy and Public Affairs*, *12*, 3–33
Cooper, J. (1977) 'Aristotle on the Forms of Friendship', *Review of Metaphysics*, *30*, 619–48
Blom-Cooper, L. and Drewry, G. (eds.) (1976) *Law and Morality: A Reader*, London
Cooper, N. (1971) 'Oughts and Wants', in G. Mortimore (ed.), *Weakness of Will*, London
Crittenden, B. (1978) 'Autonomy as an Aim of Education', in K. Strike and K. Egan (eds.), *Ethics and Educational Policy*, London
Crocker, L. (1980) *Positive Liberty*, The Hague
Daniels, N. (ed.) (1976) *Reading Rawls*, New York
Davidson, D. (1969) 'How Is Weakness of the Will Possible?', in J. Feinberg (ed.), *Moral Concepts*, Oxford
—— (1982) 'Paradoxes of Irrationality', in R. Wollheim and J. Hopkins (eds.), *Philosophical Essays on Freud*, Cambridge
Day, J.P. (1970) 'On Liberty and the Real Will', *Philosophy*, *45*, 177–92
Dearden, R.F. (1972) 'Autonomy and Education', in R.F. Dearden, P.H. Hirst and R.S. Peters (eds.), *Education and the Development of Reason*, London
—— (1975) 'Autonomy as an Educational Ideal', in S. Brown (ed.), *Philosophers Discuss Education*, London
Devlin, P. (1965) *The Enforcement of Morals*, Oxford
Downie, R.S. and Telfer, E. (1971) 'Autonomy', *Philosophy*, *46*, 293–301
Dworkin, G. (1970) 'Acting Freely', *Nous*, *4*, 367–83
—— (1972) 'Paternalism', *The Monist*, *56*, 64–84
—— (1976) 'Autonomy and Behaviour Control', *Hastings Center Report*, *6*, 23–8
—— (1978) 'Moral Autonomy', in H.T. Engelhardt, Jr., and D. Callahan (eds.), *Morals, Science and Sociality*, Hastings-on-Hudson, N.Y.
—— (1981) 'The Concept of Autonomy', *Grazer Philosophische Studien*, *12–13*, 203–13
—— (1983) 'Paternalism: Some Second Thoughts', in R. Sartorius (ed.) *Paternalism*, Minneapolis
Dworkin, R. (1968) 'Lord Devlin and the Enforcement of Morals', in J.J. Thomson and G. Dworkin (eds.), *Ethics*, New York
—— (1977) *Taking Rights Seriously*, Cambridge, Mass.
—— (1978) 'Liberalism', in S. Hampshire (ed.), *Public and Private Morality*, Cambridge
Easton, L. (1981) 'Marx and Individual Freedom', *The Philosophical Forum*, *12*, 193–213
Esheté, A. (1982) 'Character, Virtue and Freedom', *Philosophy*, *57*, 495–513
Feinberg, J. (1971) 'Legal Paternalism', *Canadian Journal of Philosophy*, *1*, 105–24
—— (1973) *Social Philosophy*, Englewood Cliffs, N.J.
—— (1973a) '"Harmless Immoralities" and Offensive Nuisances', in N.S. Care and K.T. Trelogan (eds.), *Issues in Law and Morality*, Cleveland and London
—— (1975) 'Limits to the Free Expression of Opinion', in J. Feinberg and H. Gross (eds.), *Philosophy of Law*, Encino and Belmont, CA
—— (1977) 'Harm and Self-Interest', in P.M.S. Hacker and J. Raz (eds.), *Law, Morality and Society*, Oxford
—— (1978) 'The Interest in Liberty on the Scales', in A. Goldman and J. Kim (eds.), *Values and Morals*, Dordrecht, Holland
—— (1979) 'Behaviour Control: Freedom and Behaviour Control', in W.T. Reich (ed.),

The Encyclopedia of Bioethics, New York, vol. 1
—— (1979a) 'Pornography and the Criminal Law', *University of Pittsburgh Law Review*, 40, 567–651
—— (1980) 'Absurd Self-Fulfilment: An Essay on the Merciful Perversity of the Gods', in P. van Inwagen (ed.), *Time and Cause: Essays Presented to Richard Taylor*, Dordrecht, Holland
—— (1980a) 'The Child's Right to an Open Future', in W. Aiken and H. La Follette (eds.), *Whose Child?: Children's Rights, Parental Authority and State Power*, Totowa, N.J.
—— (1980b) *Rights, Justice and the Bounds of Liberty*, Princeton, N.J.
—— (1984-) *The Moral Limits of the Criminal Law*, Oxford
Fingarette, H. (1969) *Self Deception*, London
Fleming, N. (1981) 'Autonomy of the Will', *Mind*, 90, 201–23
Fotion, N. (1979) 'Paternalism', *Ethics*, 89, 191–210
Fowler, M. (1980) 'Stability and Utopia: A Critique of Nozick's Framework Argument', *Ethics*, 90, 550–63
Frankfurt, H. (1971) 'Freedom of the Will and the Concept of a Person' *Journal of Philosophy*, 68, 5–20
—— (1973) 'Coercion and Moral Responsibility', in T. Honderich (ed.), *Essays on Freedom of Action*, London
—— (1976) 'Identification and Externality', in A. Rorty (ed.), *The Identities of Persons*, Berkeley, CA
—— (1982) 'The Importance of What We Care About', *Synthese*, 53, 257–72
Freud, S. (1953–1966) 'Introductory Lectures on Psycho-Analysis'; 'Notes Upon a Case of Obsessional Neurosis'; 'Inhibitions, Symptoms and Anxiety'; volumes 15–16, 20 and 22 respectively in *The Standard Edition of the Complete Psychological Works of Sigmund Freud*, J. Strachey *et al.* (eds.), London
Fried, C. (1970) *An Anatomy of Values: Problems of Personal and Social Choice*, Cambridge, MA
Friedman, M. (1962) *Capitalism and Freedom*, Chicago
—— and Friedman, R. (1980) *Free to Choose: A Personal Statement*, New York
Garry, A. (1978) 'Pornography and Respect for Women', *Social Theory and Practice*, 4, 395–421
Gert, B. and Culver, C. (1976) 'Paternalistic Behaviour', *Philosophy and Public Affairs*, 6, 45–57
—— (1979) 'The Justification of Paternalism', *Ethics*, 89, 370–90
Glover, J. (1977) *Causing Death and Saving Lives*, Harmondsworth
Gould, C. (1978) *Marx's Social Ontology: Individuality and Community in Marx's Theory of Social Reality*, Cambridge, MA
Gray, J. (1983) *Mill on Liberty: A Defence*, London
Green, T.H. (1906) 'Lecture on "Liberal Legislation and Freedom of Contract"', in Vol. III of *Works of T.H. Green*, London
Greenspan, P. (1980) 'A Case of Mixed Feelings: Ambivalence and the Logic of Emotion', in A. Rorty (ed.), *Explaining Emotions*, Berkeley, CA
Greenstein, F. (1965) *Children and Politics*, New Haven
Gross, H. (1971) 'Privacy and Autonomy', *Nomos XIII: Privacy*, J.W. Chapman and J.R. Pennock (eds.), New York
—— (1979) *A Theory of Criminal Justice*, New York
Gutmann, A. (1980) *Liberal Equality*, Cambridge
—— (1980a) 'Children, Paternalism and Education', *Philosophy and Public Affairs*, 9, 338–58
Haksar, V. (1979) *Equality, Liberty and Perfectionism*, Oxford
Hamlyn, D.W. (1971) 'Self Deception', *Proceedings of the Aristotelian Society, Supplementary Volume*, 45, 61–72
Hampshire, S. (1965) *Freedom of the Individual*, London

—— (1978) 'On Having a Reason', in G. Vesey (ed.), *Human Values: Royal Institute of Philosophy Lectures, 11*, Sussex, UK

Hancock, R. (1974) *Twentieth Century Ethics*, New York and London

Harris, C.E. (1977) 'Paternalism and the Enforcement of Morality', *South-Western Journal of Philosophy, 8*, 85–93

Harris, J. (1974) 'The Marxist Conception of Violence', *Philosophy and Public Affairs, 3*, 192–220

—— (1980) *Violence and Responsibility*, London

—— (1982) 'Bad Samaritans Cause Harm', *Philosophical Quarterly, 32*, 60–69

Hart, H.L.A. (1963) *Law, Liberty and Morality*, Oxford

—— and Honoré, A.M. (1959) *Causation in the Law*, Oxford

Hayek, F. (1960) *The Constitution of Liberty*, Chicago

—— (1973) *Law, Legislation and Liberty*, Vol. I, Chicago

—— (1976) *Law, Legislation and Liberty*, Vol. II, Chicago

—— (1979) *Law, Legislation and Liberty*, Vol. III, Chicago

Hill, S.B. (1979) 'Self-Determination and Autonomy', in R. Wasserstrom (ed.), *Today's Moral Problems*, New York

Hodson, J. (1977) 'The Principle of Paternalism', *American Philosophical Quarterly, 14*, 61–9

Hospers, J. (1958) 'What Means This Freedom?', in S. Hook (ed.), *Determinism and Freedom in the Age of Modern Science*, New York

—— (1980) 'Libertarianism and Legal Paternalism', *Journal of Libertarian Studies, 4*, 255–65

Husak, D. (1980) 'Paternalism and Autonomy', *Philosophy and Public Affairs, 10*, 27–46

Kant, I. *Foundations of the Metaphysics of Morals*

Keat, R. (1982) 'Liberal Rights and Socialism', in K. Graham (ed.), *Contemporary Political Philosophy: Radical Studies*, Cambridge

King, P. (1976) *Toleration*, London

Kleinig, J. (1976) 'Good Samaritanism', *Philosophy and Public Affairs, 5*, 382–407

—— (1979) 'Consent as a Defence in Criminal Law', *Archiv für Rechts- und Sozialphilosophie, 65*, 329–44

—— (1983) *Paternalism*, Totowa, N.J.

Kuflick, A. (1984) 'The Inalienability of Autonomy', *Philosophy and Public Affairs, 13*, 271–98

Ladenson, R.F. (1975) 'A Theory of Personal Autonomy', *Ethics, 86*, 30–48

—— (1977) 'Mill's Conception of Individuality', *Social Theory and Practice, 4*, 167–82

La Follette, H. (1978) 'Why Libertarianism is Mistaken', in J. Arthur and W.H. Shaw (eds.), *Justice and Economic Distribution*, Englewood Cliffs, N.J.

Lewis, C.I. (1946) *Theory of Knowledge and Valuation*, La Salle, Illinois

Liddell, H. and Scott, R. (1897) *A Greek-English Lexicon*, New York

Locke, D. and Frankfurt, H. (1975) 'Three Concepts of Free Action', *Proceedings of the Aristotelian Society, Supplementary Volume, 49*, 95–125

Locke, J. (1963) *Second Treatise on Government* in *Two Treatises on Government*, P. Laslett (ed.), Cambridge

Loevinsohn, E. (1977) 'Liberty and the Redistribution of Property', *Philosophy and Public Affairs, 6*, 226–39

Lucas, J.R. (1966) *The Principles of Politics*, Oxford

MacCallum, G. (1967) 'Negative and Positive Freedom', *Philosophical Review, 76*, 312–34

McCloskey, H.J. (1970) 'Liberty of Expression: Its Grounds and Limits I', *Inquiry, 13*, 219–37

—— (1971) *John Stuart Mill: A Critical Study*, London

—— (1980) 'Privacy and the Right to Privacy', *Philosophy, 55*, 17–38

McDermott. F.E. (1975) 'Against the Persuasive Definition of "Self-Determination" ', in F.E. McDermott (ed.), *Self-Determination in Social Work*, London

Mack, E. (1978) 'Liberty and Justice' in J. Arthur and W.H. Shaw (eds.), *Justice and Economic Distribution*, Englewood Cliffs, N.J.

—— (1980) 'Bad Samaritanism and the Causation of Harm', *Philosophy and Public Affairs*,

9, 230–59

Macpherson, C.B. (1977) 'Human Rights as Property Rights', *Dissent*, *24*, 72–7

May, L. (1980) 'Paternalism and Self-Interest', *Journal of Value Inquiry*, *14*, 195–216

Meiklejohn, A. (1965) *Political Freedom*, New York

Mill, J.S. (1963–   ) *Principles of Political Economy*, 'Chapters on Socialism', in *Essays on Economy and Society* and *On Liberty* in *Essays on Politics and Society*, vols. 2–3, 4–5 and 18, respectively, of *Collected Works of J.S. Mill*, J.M. Robson (ed.), Toronto

Mischel, T. (1970) 'Understanding Neurotic Behaviour: From "Mechanism" to "Intentionality"', in T. Mischel (ed.), *Understanding Other Persons*, Oxford

Mitchell, B. (1967) *Law, Morality and Religion*, Oxford

Monro, D.H. (1970) 'Liberty of Expression: Its Grounds and Limits II', *Inquiry*, *13*, 238–53

Moore, G.E. (1903) *Principia Ethica*, Cambridge

—— (1911) *Ethics*, London

—— (1962) 'Is Goodness a Quality?', in *Philosophical Papers*, New York

—— (1968) 'A Reply to my Critics', in P. Schilpp (ed.), *The Philosophy of G.E. Moore*, La Salle, Illinois

Mortimore, G. (ed.) (1971) *Weakness of Will*, London

Murphy, J. (1974) 'Incompetence and Paternalism', *Archiv für Rechts- und Sozialphilosophie*, *60*, 465–86

—— (1975) 'Total Institutions and the Possibility of Consent to Organic Therapies', *Human Rights*, *5*, 25–45

Nagel, T. (1979) *Mortal Questions*, Cambridge

Narveson, J. (1976) 'A Puzzle About Economic Justice in Rawls' Theory', *Social Theory and Practice*, *4*, 1–28

Neely, W. (1974) 'Freedom and Desire', *Philosophical Review*, *83*, 32–54

Newton, L. (1981) 'Liberty and Laetrile: Implications of Right of Access', *Journal of Value Inquiry*, *15*, 55–67

Norman, R. (1982) 'Does Equality Destroy Liberty?', in K. Graham (ed.) *Contemporary Political Philosophy: Radical Studies*, Cambridge

Norton, D. (1977) 'Individualism and Productive Justice', *Ethics*, *87*, 113–25

Nozick, R. (1969) 'Coercion', in S. Morgenbesser, P. Suppes and M. White (eds.), *Philosophy, Science and Method*, New York

—— (1974) *Anarchy, State, and Utopia*, Oxford

O'Neill, O. (1979) 'The Most Extensive Liberty', *Proceedings of the Aristotelian Society*, *80*, 45–59

Oppenheim, F. (1981) *Political Concepts: A Reconstruction*, Oxford

Parent, W. (1974) 'Some Recent Work on the Concept of Liberty', *American Philosophical Quarterly*, *11*, 149–67

Paul, J. (ed.) (1981) *Reading Nozick: Essays on 'Anarchy, State, and Utopia'*, Totowa, N.J.

Pears, D. (1984) *Motivated Irrationality*, Oxford

Penelhum, T. (1971) 'The Importance of Self-Identity', *Journal of Philosophy*, *68*, 667–77

—— (1979) 'Human Nature and External Desires', *The Monist*, *62*, 304–19

Pennock, J.R. and Chapman, J.W. (eds.) (1972) *Nomos XIV: Coercion*, New York

Peters, R.S. (1973) 'Freedom and the Development of the Free Man', in J.F. Doyle (ed.) *Educational Judgements*, London

Pierce, C. (1975) 'Hart on Paternalism', *Analysis*, *35*, 205–7

Plamenatz, J. (1968) *Consent, Freedom and Political Obligation*, London

Plato *The Republic*

Poole, R. (1975) 'Freedom and Alienation', *Radical Philosophy*, no. 12, 11–17

Rachels, J. (1975) 'Why Privacy Is Important', *Philosophy and Public Affairs*, *4*, 323–33

Rawls, J. (1971) *A Theory of Justice*, Cambridge, MA

—— (1980) 'Rational and Full Autonomy', *Journal of Philosophy*, *77*, 515–35

Raz, J. (1982) 'Liberation, Autonomy and the Politics of Neutral Concern', *Midwest Studies in Philosophy*, *7*, 89–120

Young, G. (1978) 'Justice and Capitalist Production', *Canadian Journal of Philosophy*, 8, 421–58

Young, R. (1975) *Freedom, Responsibility and God*, London and New York

—— (1976) 'Voluntary and Nonvoluntary Euthanasia', *The Monist*, 59, 264–83

—— (1977) 'Revolutionary Terrorism, Crime and Morality', *Social Theory and Practice*, 4, 287–302

—— (1979) 'Compatibilism and Conditioning', *Nous*, 13, 461–78

—— (1980) 'Population Control, Coercion and Morality', in D.S. Mannison, M.A. McRobbie and R.Routley (eds.), *Environmental Philosophy*, Canberra

—— (1980a) 'The Environment, Human Welfare and Economic Growth', in D.S. Mannison, M.A. McRobbie and R. Routley (eds.), *Environmental Philosophy*, Canberra

—— (1980b) 'In the Interests of Children and Adolescents', in W. Aiken and H. La Follette (eds.), *Whose Child?: Children's Rights, Parental Authority and State Power*, Totowa, N.J.

Zimmerman, D. (1981) 'Coercive Wage Offers', *Philosophy and Public Affairs*, 10, 121–45

INDEX